NALU

NALU

HISTORY, LEGENDS, AND WISDOM FROM 1,000 YEARS OF HAWAIIAN SURFING

MARIE ALOHALANI BROWN
AND IAN LENDLER

Clarkson Potter/Publishers
New York

MAB—

To my ocean-loving children and granddaughter,
Lehua, Cristoforo Kekoapono, and Penelope Pono—
and to my Kanaka ʻŌiwi kūpuna.

IL—

To my grandmother,
who took me to the beach every day.

CONTENTS

H a w a
Hanalei B.
KAUAI
Haena
Kahala Pt
Kaulakahi Channel
Lehua
5170
Nawiliwili B.
Lihue
Nonopapa
Niihau
Port Allen
Kaula
Kauai Channel
OAHU
Waialua
Kaena Pt
Waipahu
Pearl Harbour
HAWAII
SCALE : 1 INCH TO 98 MILES
0
50
100 Miles

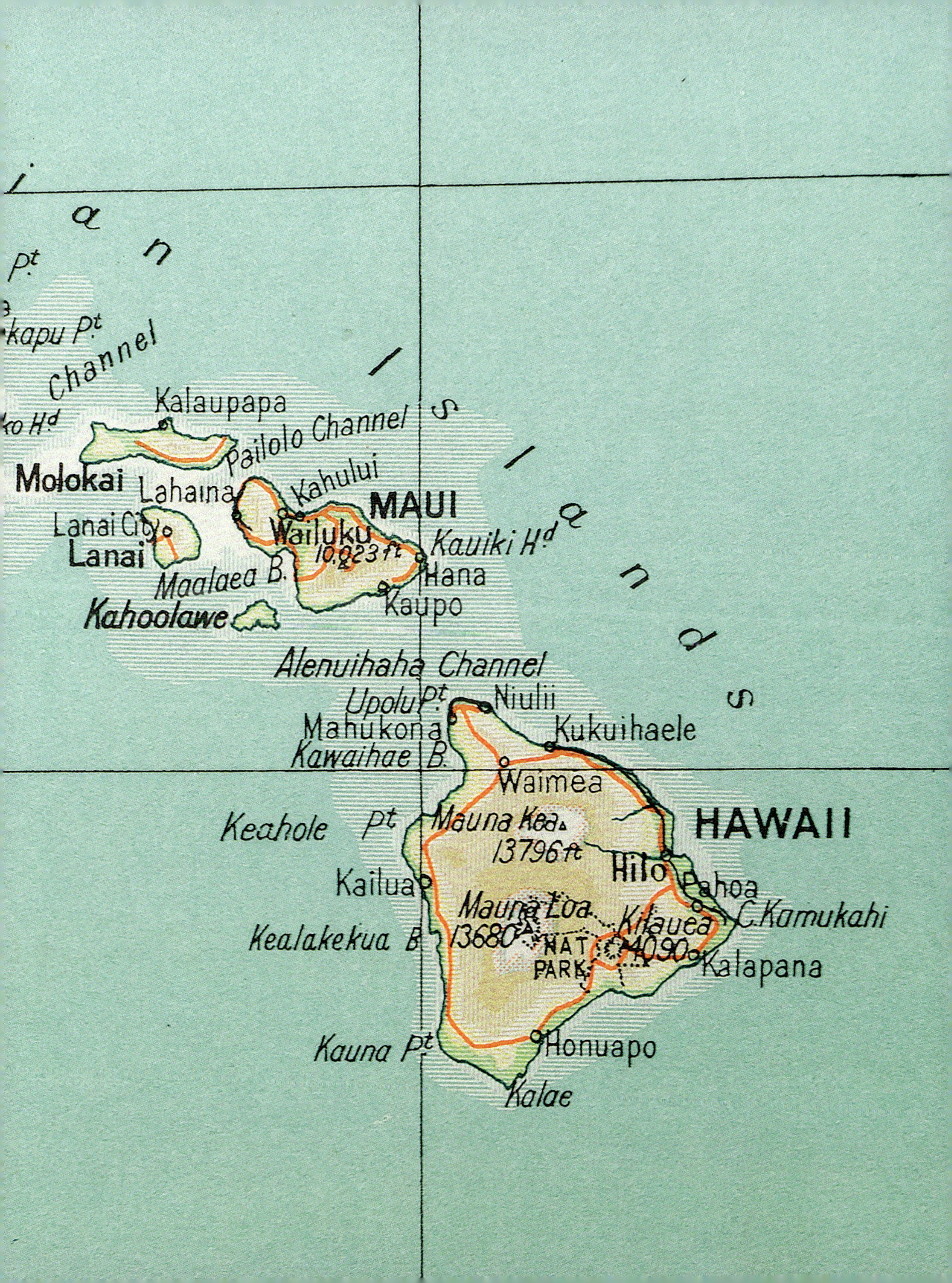

Hawaiian Islands
Pt
kapu Pt
Channel
ko Hd
Kalaupapa
Pailolo Channel
Molokai
Lahaina
Kahului
MAUI
Lanai City
Lanai
Wailuku
10,023 ft
Kauiki Hd
Hana
Maalaea B.
Kaupo
Kahoolawe
Alenuihaha Channel
Upolu Pt
Niulii
Mahukona
Kukuihaele
Kawaihae B.
Waimea
Keahole Pt
Mauna Kea
13796 ft
HAWAII
Hilo
Pahoa
Kailua
Mauna Loa
13680
Kilauea
C. Kamukahi
Kealakekua B.
NAT PARK
4090
Kalapana
Kauna Pt
Honuapo
Kalae

INTRODUCTION

In Hawai'i, November is known as 'Ikuā, the month of deafening noise. 'Ikuā (which means noisy, din, clamorous) is the time of year when the voices of the gods resound across the islands through the elements. Storms churn the sea into enormous waves that pound the shore, filling villages with their rumbling. Howling winds, drumming rains, and booming thunder rattle people's homes.

The people of Ni'ihau celebrated the arrival of 'Ikuā, because it meant big-wave season had arrived. They held a pā'ina (feast) on the beach. Before they ate, an elder said a prayer and gave a food bundle to a man, who paddled his board past the surf break. He opened the bundle, and as he fed the ocean its share of food, the ocean calmed. But after it fed, the ocean would send a large wave so the man could surf back to shore. Only then could everyone eat and play in the water. The celebration lasted from one to three weeks—day and night, they ate, sang, swam, and surfed in the ocean. After all, ua pi'i ka nalu (surf was up)!

Every culture has spring and harvest festivals, but how many can say they have a festival for good surf season? Hawaiians didn't call it surfing, though. The entire culture of surfing, as Westerners know it today, has only been around for about a hundred years. Even the word *surfing* is a Western invention created by early visitors to Hawai'i in the late 1800s, when they tried to describe Hawaiians riding waves. They didn't know Hawaiians already had a name for it—he'e nalu, wave sliding.

He'e nalu is an ancient sport, at least a thousand years old. But for Hawaiians, it is more than just a sport or recreation. It is an integral part of their society. He'e nalu has its own holidays, rituals, altars, and mythology. When the waves were right (and in Hawai'i, they're right more often than anywhere else), entire villages abandoned their duties to play in the ocean. Men, women, and children would dive in to ride, compete, socialize, and flirt. Kings and queens claimed the best waves for themselves. Crafting a board was surrounded by ritual.

Polynesian cultures are the only ones in the world with gods who surf, and Hawaiian gods could totally rip. They challenged each other to surf competitions and surfed to seduce mortals. One goddess caught waves by riding her tongue!

For a thousand years, Hawaiians lived the philosophy every surfer knows to be true: When the waves are good, why would you want to do anything else?

Over a millennium, Hawaiians have built a vast body of surfing lore—language, proverbs, stories, and advice. It is indisputably the greatest surfing culture in history. But you wouldn't know it by looking at modern surfing culture. Sure, films and magazines pay tribute to Hawai'i and its famous waves. Every surfer in the world throws the Hawaiian shaka hand gesture.

Beyond that, though, how much "Hawaiianness" is actually in Western surfing culture? Almost none.

How did this ancient indigenous sport come to be associated with blond Southern Californians? Surfing is an immigrant story. It came to America from a foreign land with a foreign name: It arrived as he'e nalu in the early 1900s, introduced by Hawaiians who found themselves in places like Santa Cruz and San Diego and who missed the aquatic joys of home. But modern surfing culture truly began in post–World War II Southern California, when it exploded into pop culture (movies, music, magazines) and spread to the rest of the world. Unfortunately, when he'e nalu transitioned into surfing, a lot was lost in translation.

This wasn't entirely deliberate. Much of Hawai'i's cultural knowledge just wasn't available to anyone outside the islands. Hawai'i has a rich storytelling tradition, but to know the stories, you had to hear them firsthand, and you had to understand Hawaiian. Once the Hawaiian Kingdom began publishing newspapers, Hawaiians filled the pages with knowledge on every topic, including surfing. But you had to be able to read Hawaiian. Since then, only a *fraction* of that knowledge has been translated into English. Whatever is floating around on the internet today about Hawaiian culture, including surfing, is based on endless rehashing of what little has been translated.

If you were a kid living in San Diego in the 1950s and you picked up a surfboard for the first time, you had no history or deeper culture to look to for guidance. In the absence of Hawaiian knowledge, surfing became American. The first generation of American surfers created their own culture with their own values, sometimes for the worse. Some of modern surfing's most toxic traits are Western inventions. One of the most glaring divides between Hawaiian and Westernized surfing culture is the past century's notion that "girls can't surf."

Lahaina, Maui, 1855

Thankfully, that idea has been dying off in recent because it goes completely against Hawaiian culture. Hawaiians celebrated the exceptional skills and style of female surfers. In fact, in their myths, it was goddesses who laid the smackdown on men who thought they could surf better.

In modern surfing culture, fighting over waves is a constant conflict. But the Hawaiians of old loved sharing waves. When multiple people rode a wave, they often raised their arms like wings to resemble a flock of birds skimming the water. When kāne (man, men) and wāhine (women; *singular* wahine) found someone attractive, they rode the same wave to flirt with them.

The biggest difference between surfing's Hawaiian roots and its modern American version is that modern surfers became a variation of the American icon—photos show the rugged individual, the lone ocean cowboy, sun-soaked or storm-tossed, staring out to sea (although every surfer knows that just out of the photo's frame, there are about thirty other people in the lineup).

In 1950s America, if you spent your life on the water rather than joining the rat race and "getting ahead," you were bohemian, living outside the bounds of society.

But in Hawai'i, a life dedicated to the ocean didn't mean separating yourself from society. It *was* society. He'e nalu was a joyous, communal, family activity. It was born out of one of the greatest water cultures in human history.

THE THATCH HOUSES OF A WHOLE VILLAGE STOOD EMPTY. . . . DAILY TASKS SUCH AS FARMING, FISHING, AND TAPA-MAKING WERE LEFT UNDONE WHILE AN ENTIRE COMMUNITY—MEN, WOMEN, AND CHILDREN—ENJOYED THEMSELVES IN THE RISING SURF AND RUSHING WHITE WATER.

—WILLIAM ELLIS, MISSIONARY, HAWAI'I ISLAND (1820)

Surfers (from left to right): Kaika, Kawika, Keahi, and unidentified. This is one of the earliest surfing photos ever taken in Ni'ihau in 1890. The Sinclair-Robinson family has owned the island since 1864, when they purchased it for $10,000 from the Hawaiian monarchy. In 1915, they closed it to outsiders to preserve Hawaiian culture and protect the residents from infectious diseases.

Beginning around 1000 BCE, Polynesians explored the world's largest ocean using nothing but canoes and their knowledge of the stars, winds, waves, and sky. Sailing for weeks and months at a time, they discovered and settled the most remote islands on earth. This required a profound comfort with the ocean. They were born on the water, lived on the water, and died on the water. They spent their lives looking at, listening to, and moving with the water. When swells became waves that finally broke on new lands, those waves held no mystery. The voyagers knew their rhythm well—how to move and thrive inside of them, how to catch a wave and slide.

There are many great water cultures in the world, all of whom have a deep comfort with the movements of the ocean. But only the Polynesians crafted equipment with the sole purpose of riding a wave for fun. Yet it was in Hawai'i that surfing truly flourished. Why?

History is one factor. Hawai'i was one of the last island chains settled by Polynesians. By the time the first settlers arrived from the area known today as French Polynesia—notably Tahiti, Bora Bora, Tuamotu, Te Henua 'Enata (the Marquesas Islands)—they came with centuries of wave-riding experience. Geography is another factor. Tahiti has famously spectacular waves, but coral reefs limit their accessibility. There are only so many places you can surf unless you want to paddle out for half a mile or risk getting slammed onto a razor-sharp reef. Hawai'i, on the other hand, is a planetary miracle for making waves. There are surf breaks *everywhere*—breaks that are easy to reach, reef breaks, sand breaks, point breaks, river breaks. . . . Every man, woman, and child can find a wave that works for them. Hawai'i was at a crossroads of time and place to be the perfect laboratory for developing surfing—board shapes, sizes, and riding styles—as an art form.

Many books try to describe the joy of surfing—to explain why surfers put up with the wave-pounding, face-planting, and near drownings that accompany almost every session.

Writers reach for ancient philosophies. There are books on the Zen of surfing, the dharma of surfing, soul-surfing, the science of surfing. But none have tried to understand surfing through the eyes and minds of the people who gave birth to the sport. Compare surfing to other activities that share such a deep connection to their society. One beginner karate class will introduce you to Japanese language and values. The same is true for yoga and Indian culture. Learning the mother culture of an activity is an integral and spiritual part of that practice. The benefits go beyond cultural respect; the culture that births an activity usually has greater insight into it.

Over the years, Westerners have adopted many Hawaiian water skills without recognizing their origins. Duke Kahanamoku introduced the flutter kick (the style you probably learned in childhood swimming lessons) when he dominated Olympic swimming in the 1910s and '20s. The concept of lifeguards and the use of longboards for water rescue come from Hawai'i. And of course, he'e nalu is the origin of the entire $25 billion board-sport industry. Surfers, skateboarders, and snowboarders owe their thanks to the Hawaiian people.

For too long, surfing has been missing too much of its history. That's where this book comes in. It draws upon a thousand years' worth of surfing stories, proverbs, customs, advice, gods, and legends from the people who perfected the sport. But this is not just a history book. It is a living document that captures the water culture of Hawai'i. Many people today earn their living as lifeguards (some of the best on earth), boat captains, board makers, pro surfers, surf photographers, and more. Many descend from long lines of legendary watermen and -women. *Nalu* recognizes the rich tradition that has always been surfing's birthright.

However, this book is not just for surfers. It is for anyone who feels a connection to the ocean. It offers a chance to experience the ocean in a brand-new way, through the eyes of the first people of surfing.

Cliff Kapono, somewhere on Hawai'i Island

A quintessential aspect of Hawaiian culture is something known as "talking story." It can be as simple as a conversation between friends and family or telling stories about gods and culturally important places. Hawaiian culture has many tales of mythological figures who surf, so we include a "talk story" tour of surf legends around the islands. Because you will encounter many mythological characters in this book, we provide a glossary to guide you (see Mythological Characters, page 292).

Kanaka 'Ōiwi (Hawaiian) coauthor Marie Alohalani Brown grew up in Mākaha immersed in these stories. Her journey as cultural practitioner—from a childhood spent in the ocean bodysurfing and bodyboarding to studying under Tom "Pōhaku" Stone, surfing, and paddling for a canoe club to becoming a professor of Hawaiian religion and a Hawaiian-language translator—highlights the deep-rooted ties between her personal history, cultural identity, and academic pursuit. She has dedicated her

Riders (from right to left): Tiana Ahue, Ha'aheo Foster-Blomfield, Pomai Hoapili, and Bonga Perkins (steersman). Mākaha, O'ahu.

life to studying and promoting Hawaiian history, culture, and religion.

Coauthor Ian Lendler has loved the ocean and being on, in, or under the water since he was a child. When he and Alohalani became friends, they shared stories about their mutual love of surfing and ocean life. Born and raised on the East Coast, Ian knew little about Hawaiian culture, but the curiosity and love of a good story that shaped his career as a writer and journalist led him to explore surfing's Hawaiian roots. To Alohalani's amusement, he kept presenting her with information he'd found on the internet that was misinformed, mistranslated, and sometimes just completely made up. Over many afternoons (and a few beers), she corrected and taught him about real Hawaiian culture. Eventually, these talks (her knowledge, his excitement, and their shared love of nerding out on history and literature) became the basis for this book.

E hele mai e 'au. Come swim with us.

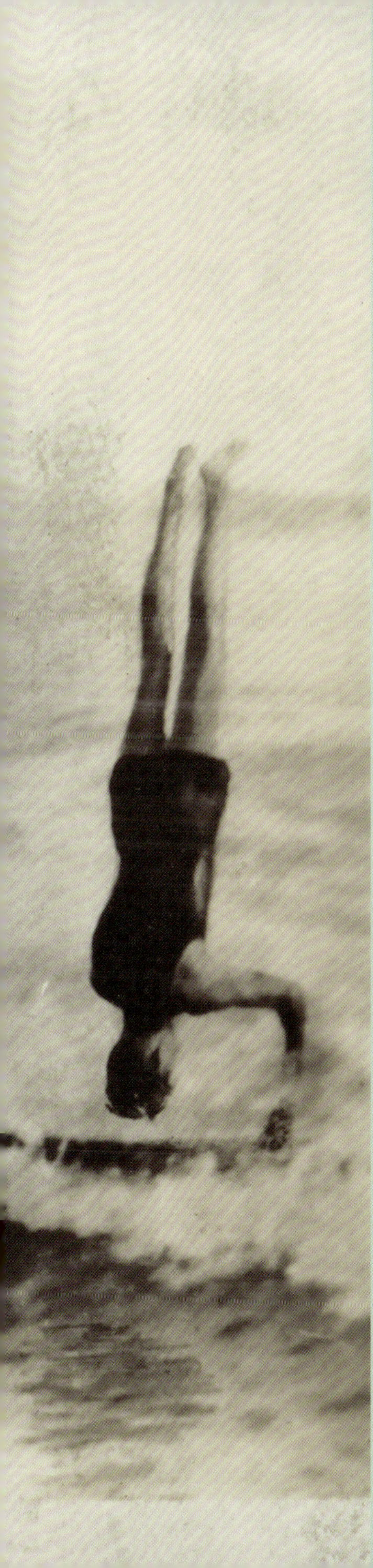

PRONUNCIATION GUIDE

Hawaiian words, names, and syllables always end in a vowel. The alphabet has thirteen letters: a, e, i, o, u, h, k, l, m, n, p, w, '). The last letter is a glottal stop termed *'okina*. Current orthography also uses a kahakō (macron) to mark long vowels.

Aloha: Ah-low-hah (*not* ah-low-wah)

He'e nalu: Heh-eh nah-loo

O'ahu: Oh-ah-who (*not* oh-wah-who)

Hawai'i: Hah-why-ee (*not* hah-why)

Honolulu: Ho-no-loo-loo (*not* ha-na-loo-loo)

Kaua'i: Cow-wah-ee (*not* cow-why)

Kupuna and kūpuna: Coo-poo-nah (*not* kah-poo-nah) and Coooo-poo-nah

Menehune: Meh-neh-who-neh

Kamehameha: Kah-may-hah-may-hah (*not* kah-may-yah-may-yah)

Ka'ahumanu: Kah-ah-who-mah-new

Pele: Peh-leh (*not* Pay-lay)

Hi'iakaikapoliopele: Hee-ee-ah-kah-ee-kah-poh-lee-oh-peh-leh

Previous: Marcus Hickman at Pipeline during the Da Hui Backdoor Shootout in January 2008. Veteran photographer Sean Davey explains, "This was a northwest set lighting up the inside reefs while a new north swell fired across the outside reef, creating what is the only time that I have seen all Pipeline reefs break at the same time."

Left: Waikīkī circa 1910

PART I

KE KUMU

THE FOUNDATION

Ho'okipa, Maui

WATER

Polynesia, meaning "many islands," is defined by its connection to the sea. The first Polynesians emerged around 2000 BCE in coastal Southeast Asia, where they developed advanced seafaring skills that transformed the ocean into a means of connection rather than separation. For generations, they lived intimately with the ocean as they voyaged to the far corners of the Polynesian Triangle, an 800,000-square-mile area demarcated by Hawai'i, Rapa Nui (Easter Island), and Aotearoa (New Zealand). By around 400 CE, they had reached the most isolated place on earth—the Hawaiian Islands.

Over thousands of years, Polynesian lives, languages, cultures, and religions were shaped by the ocean and by what marine biologist Wallace Nichols called the "Blue Mind"—the physical and psychological state of well-being humans experience when in the presence of water. Water is one of nature's most powerful forces. For Hawaiians, it is both an akua (deity) and a kupuna (ancestor, *plural* kūpuna). Their grasp of water's ever-changing nature is expressed in akua mo'o (lizard, reptile), who personify freshwater. Mo'o shapeshift, and so does water. Both are simultaneously life-giving and death-dealing. No water, no life.

WAI AND KAI

Most English-speaking people don't tend to think of "water" as an idea, but it is. For Hawaiians, the word *water* is so vague that it's impractical. The differences between freshwater and saltwater are so important that it doesn't make sense to lump them together. Wai is freshwater. Kai is seawater. Wai kai is brackish water, where wai and kai mix. Wai is essential for life and kai informs Hawaiian identity—a means of travel and a source of food and medicine, healing, and recreation. Despite their obvious differences, wai and kai are also deeply connected. Hawaiians think of them as twin akua—Kāne and Kanaloa.

Kāne embodies the sun, rain (source of freshwater), clouds, rainbows (and much more).

Kanaloa personifies the ocean, ocean currents, and ocean winds.

As twin brothers, they represent the holistic nature of the water cycle itself. Kāne is the elder twin. In this respect, Hawaiian knowledge parallels the scientific understanding that all water on earth first came into being when the earth's molten core began to cool and release vapor, which condensed into a rain that fell nonstop for millions of years. We drink and swim in the same waters as the dinosaurs and our earliest human ancestors.

Hawaiian and scientific mutual understanding of the ocean's behavior does not stop there. Waves are born from the water cycle. The ocean's energy comes from the sun, which heats the water. The evaporation rises and cools into clouds that release rain to the sea. Is it any wonder then that Kāne is the sun, rain, and clouds at the same time? When Kāne's storms drum upon the surface of Kanaloa's ocean, these brothers create waves that ripple out worldwide and break on every shore. So when you ride a wave, you connect directly to the power of these akua.

ALOHA ʻĀINA, ALOHA KAI

According to Hawaiians, the island world has three realms: ʻāina (land), kai (sea), and lani (sky). Akua are the natural phenomena that animate these realms. For countless generations, Hawaiians lived in close connection to this world, observed it, and claimed kinship with it. Hawaiians are part of a vast web in which land, sea, and sky and everything therein are revered kūpuna.

ʻĀina is often translated as *land*, but its literal meaning is "that which feeds." Because the ʻāina and kai feed us, we have a responsibility to treat them with aloha. Aloha is a complex idea that has no equivalent in English. You need more than forty English words to express its many nuances: love, affection, compassion, mercy, sympathy, pity, kindness, sentiment, grace, charity; greeting, salutation, regards; sweetheart, lover, loved one; beloved, loving, kind, compassionate, charitable, lovable; to love, be fond of; to show kindness, mercy, pity, charity, affection; to venerate; to remember with affection; to greet.

Kiʻi (images of gods) of Kāne and Kanaloa at the Puʻuhonua o Hōnaunau (City of Refuge) in South Kona, Hawaiʻi Island

The deep-seated love Hawaiians feel for their islands is expressed in the well-known phrase and philosophy "aloha ʻāina." They recognize that land, sea, and sky are connected. The land does not stop at the ocean's edge but extends beneath it. The sky embraces them both. Therefore, aloha for the ʻāina includes aloha for kai and lani. Our actions on land affect the sea. When we fail to properly care for land and sea, we put their well-being and ours at risk.

For example, Waikīkī is one of the planet's most incredible natural amphi-theaters for surfing. Canoes, Queens, Pops, Castles, and Bowls—famous surf breaks—are all found in this one place. For a thousand years, aliʻi (members of

HE ALIʻI KA ʻĀINA; HE KAUWĀ KE KANAKA.

The land is a chief; man is its servant.

—ʻŌLELO NOʻEAU

the ruling class) chose to go there because the surfing was so good. But we will never surf the same waves as the ali'i of old.

In 1921, Honolulu city officials wanted to develop Waikīkī for tourism. The land was a marsh, with streams that emptied into the ocean, so the city dug a two-mile-long canal, the Ala Wai, to drain all that water. The streams that once flowed into the harbor inhibited coral growth, creating a natural channel. Once the freshwater was gone, coral grew, changing the shape of the ocean floor. After the canal's completion, surfers said those waves were never the same.

Aloha 'āina. Aloha kai.

Opposite, clockwise from top left: Tom "Pōhaku" Stone's blessing of Mahi, an alai'a board

Lava is a kino lau (physical manifestation) of Pele, the volcano goddess.

Bananas are a kino lau of Kanaloa.

'Ōhi'a lehua flowers are the kino lau of the forest god Kūka'ōhi'alaka and the forest goddess Hinaulu'ōhi'a.

MANA

Mana, a complex concept, informs Hawaiian ways of knowing and being. Its closest equivalent in English is *power*, but *power* does not capture its many nuances. Mana is an entity in its own right with a distinct and independent existence. Everything in nature comes into being with some degree of mana. Hawai'i's most powerful akua who personify unstoppable natural forces—Kāne (sun, freshwater, lightning, thunder, earthquakes), Kanaloa (ocean), Lono (storm clouds and raging winds), Haumea (earth), and Pele (lava)—have enormous mana.

Mana is intangible but has tangible manifestations. Mana can be spiritual, intellectual, or physical. It is behind the supernatural strength possessed by cultural heroes like Māui, but it is also found in the knowledge of master navigators on the open sea, who sense their location not just through their senses in the physical realm, but by using 'ike pāpālua (double sight) to connect to the spiritual realm. Master navigator Nainoa Thompson described this process as "knowing without knowing at all how you know."

Mana underlies the capacity for effecting positive or negative change. It is the natural ability that certain plants have to heal or kill. But it is also channeled by our words and our intentions. Practitioners of 'anā'anā, a death-dealing practice, pray people to death.

Mana can be embedded in or transferred to something else. Canoes and surfboards have multiple layers of mana. Mana is in the trees used to make them, the hands that carve and shape them, and the paddlers or surfers who ride them.

Mana can be increased or diminished. King Kamehameha I had a spittoon that he decorated with the molars of his dead enemies to insult them and their lineage. In this way, Kamehameha I increased his mana while diminishing that of his enemies.

Mana grants authority and defines status. We are all born with mana, but certain people have more than others because of their lineage. Akua have the most mana, followed by ali'i and then maka'āinana (members of the nonruling class). Abominable acts decrease your mana, but performing extraordinary feats increase it. Perfecting a skill to the point of having a nearly superhuman ability, whether in waging war, farming, or surfing, adds to your mana.

Queen's surf break in Waikīkī, circa 1924

MAI KA PIKO O KE POʻO A KA POLI O KA WĀWAE, A LAʻA MA NĀ KIHI ʻEHĀ O KE KINO.

From the crown of the head to the soles of the feet, and the four corners of the body.

—ʻŌLELO NOʻEAU

An expression used in prayers of healing. The four corners are the shoulders and hips; between them are the vital organs of the body.

OCEAN HEALING

Every surfer knows one thing to be true. You do not spend most of your time riding waves. Even the best surfers in the world can spend hours in the ocean only to ride a wave for a few seconds or not at all. So, what compels us not only to return but to crave the experience?

The simple act of being in wai or kai is the most sensual experience humans can have. Our skin is the largest organ on our body. Being caressed by saltwater reminds us of being in the ocean of our mother's womb. It is where we floated in serenity until it was time to leave her body. As soon as we breathed air, that memory began to fade from our minds . . . or did it?

Our bodies remember. The feeling—the literal, physical sensation—of the oceanic is such a powerful human experience that many cultures around the world have ritualized "being in water" in some way. Hawaiians have two such rituals: hiʻuwai and pīkai.

Opposite: Haʻa Keaulana

HI'UWAI

Hi'uwai is a ceremony of spiritual purification to prepare you for an undertaking of great importance. A hi'uwai usually takes place between midnight and dawn, often just before sunrise. You immerse your body in water to cleanse yourself spiritually, mentally, and physically. You allow your mind to rid itself of distractions, so that when you emerge from the water, you are focused on your upcoming task. Hawaiians call wai and kai the living waters of Kāne and Kanaloa because they enable life. Thus, both freshwater and saltwater can work for a hi'uwai. But because salt is a purifying element that dispels negative energy, Hawaiians use the ocean more often.

Hi'uwai are done for different reasons: birth, marriage, healing, death, or mourning. Frequently, a hi'uwai is a solemn ceremony, carried out in silence. But it can also be done for joyous events, filled with laughter and splashing. Hi'uwai may be performed with or without clothing. In the past, men, women, and children might perform the hi'uwai together without clothing. But since the arrival of Christianity, men and women tend to perform it separately.

HI'UWAI IS THE IDEA OF RETURNING BACK TO THE WOMB TO AGAIN BE INNOCENT, WITHOUT DISTRACTIONS.

—PUALANI KANAKA'OLE KANAHELE, DISTINGUISHED HULA MASTER AND SCHOLAR

For centuries, Hawaiians celebrated Makahiki, a three-month festival from mid-October to mid-January to honor Lono, the god of agriculture. It was a joyous occasion—the harvest was finished and everyone could relax. They passed the time with sports (including surfing), hula, music, and storytelling. On the first night, they lit fires near the swimming areas and immersed themselves in the ocean or streams, where they played until dawn, then left to enjoy a feast.

Hi'uwai is not a relic of the past but a living practice. When the Parks Department of Hawai'i wanted to charge visitors a fee to visit the picturesque but often crowded Hanauma Bay, they had to waive the fee for Hawaiians because it is a popular spot to hi'uwai.

Hawaiians also perform hi'uwai for events of great cultural significance. Beginning in 1941, the U.S. military used the island of Kaho'olawe for bombing practice, destroying the environment and leaving unexploded ordnance everywhere. Pressured by decades of environmental activism, in 1990, they returned Kaho'olawe to the state. Before embarking on the arduous task of restoring the island (work that continues to this day), several hundred activists and officials gathered on the island and performed a hi'uwai to "ask the island and the unseen entities to allow the cleanup to begin; that the way be open and clear."

A growing body of scientific evidence supports the health benefits of hi'uwai. Thalassotherapy, immersion in mineral-rich seawater, helps reduce inflammation, improve skin and respiratory conditions, boost the immune system, and reduce overall anxiety. Luxury hotels now offer hi'uwai ceremonies for tourists eager to experience Hawaiian spirituality.

THE HI'UWAI CEREMONY

The hi'uwai predates the creation of one of Hawai'i's most ancient and beloved tales, the epic of Hi'iakaikapoliopele (Hi'iaka for short; see page 82)—perhaps the greatest surfer in Hawaiian mythology and the youngest sister of Pele, the volcano goddess. Hi'iaka once used wai and kai to bring a man back to life by mixing the waters in a bowl and asking Lono, associated with water and healing, to bless them:

A family hi'uwai: Alvin Aiona, Iris Aiona, and June Aiona

Ē Lono! Ē Lono!!	O Lono! O Lono!!
Ē Lono kū lani	O Lono standing in the heavens
Ē Lono noho i ka wai	O Lono dwelling in the water
Ō ho'ūlu 'oe, ō 'īnana 'oe	Inspire, animate,
Hō'īana ana i ke ola	Give life to the water
Hōpu'epu'e ana 'oe i ka wai	To Kāne's water that enables life
I ka wai e ola a Kāne	To the waters indeed,
I ka wai ho'i, i ka wai ola a Kāne	To Kāne's life-giving water
Ka wai ola a Kanaloa	[To] Kanaloa's life-giving water
I ka hikina, i ke komohana	In the east, in the west
I wai hua—i wai lani	In raindrops cradled in leaves—
'Ī—ē! Holo—ē!!	sacred water
	It is said—oh! It is done—oh!!

—HI'IAKAIKAPOLIOPELE

Hanauma Bay, O'ahu

Laiana Wong Jr. performing pīkai at the Da Hui Backdoor Shootout in 2024

PĪKAI

A pīkai is performed to heal illness, to cleanse those who have done wrong or who helped prepare a corpse for burial, or to purify a dwelling of negative energy. The ritualist holds a wooden bowl filled with either seawater or salted freshwater, then uses a tī leaf to sprinkle the water over whoever or whatever needs to be purified. Surfing contests in Hawai'i often begin with a pīkai to bless surfers and their boards in order to protect them and give them strength.

THE WISDOM AND POETRY OF WATER

That Hawaiians drew wisdom from interacting with forces of nature as powerful as rain, rivers, and seas is a natural consequence of being a water people. All cultures express themselves with a common language. For Hawaiians, that is the language of water. They memorialized their water wisdom in several genres: 'ōlelo no'eau (a saying that can be poetic or didactic), oli (chants), mele (song), pule (prayers), and mo'olelo (histories). Over her lifetime, esteemed cultural expert Mary Kawena Pukui collected 'ōlelo no'eau, which she translated and explained.

He kapa malo'o wale ka 'ili. The skin is a garment that dries easily. *Being wet is nothing to worry about. Comfort with water is where Hawaiian culture begins.*

Aia nō i ke kō a ke au. Whichever way the current goes. *Time will tell.*

E 'au mālie i ke kai pāpa'u, o pakī ka wai a pula ka maka. Swim quietly in shallow water lest it splash into the eyes. *Go carefully when you are unsure of your surroundings.*

Mimiki ke kai, ahuwale ka papa leho. When the sea draws out in the tidal wave, the rocks where the cowries hide are exposed. *When you lose control of your emotions, you often reveal secrets.*

Kaiko'o ke awa, popo'i ka nalu, 'a'ohe 'ike 'ia ka po'e nāna i he'e ka nalu. The harbor is rough, the surf rolls, and the rider of the surf cannot be seen. *You don't know what will happen in times of trouble.*

La'i lua ke kai. The sea is very calm. *All is well.*

NALU

WAVES

At first there was only a raging sea

Nalu halehale, nalu ālai. Towering waves, waves that barred the way.

Then the demigod Kaulu was born. He chose to be born as a piece of rope, and his older brother Ka'eha protected him by placing him high up on a shelf where no harm could come to him. Not long after, evil spirits kidnapped Ka'eha and carried him across the ocean. That's when Kaulu changed into his human form. He had to save his brother.

Kaulu went to the shore, where the wall of towering waves barred his way. He asked the raging surf if it was strong. The surf looked down on the small child and replied with a voice that shook the earth, "I am more than strong. I am powerful."

But Kaulu was not afraid. He asked the surf why it thought it was powerful.

The surf thundered, "I strike people down."

Kaulu grabbed the surf in his hands and tore it into pieces. Then he set out on the ocean and continued his search. This is how the ocean came to have many smaller waves. It was a brother's love that made the ocean passable, that made waves that were ready to ride.

NALU ALOHA PAU ‘OLE.

Waves for which love is never-ending.

— ‘ŌLELO NO‘EAU

ANATOMY OF A WAVE

1. **Waho:** the outside, past the break.
2. **'Ale olowalu:** waves that follow one another, a set.
3. **Hānau ka nalu:** where the surf is born.
4. **Lālahalaha, 'ako'ako:** to swell up before breaking.
5. **Kua nalu:** surf just before it breaks, crest of the wave.
6. **Po'ina nalu:** surf zone, cresting of the sea, place where the sea crests and breaks.
7. **Nalu ha'i:** breaking wave.
8. **Hu'ahu'a kai:** white water, the foam from a wave that has broken. Also, **kapa kea:** literally—white blanket, the surface of the water covered by foam.

1. **'Ehu kai:** sea spray.
2. **Po'i:** lip, breaking wave.
3. **Hokua, ni'o:** peak, tip of a wave crest.
4. **'Āko'ako'a, 'ale, pū'o'akua:** wave crest, the peak.
5. **Waha (mouth), halehale nalu:** the barrel.
6. **Alo:** open face of the wave.
7. **Honua nalu, kumu nalu:** trough, base.
8. **Lala:** the shoulder, the unbroken part of the wave next to the crest.
9. **Muku, ha'i muku, lo'ulo'u:** curl.

Previous: Paumalū (Sunset Point), North Shore, O'ahu

Right, top and bottom: Pipeline, North Shore, O'ahu

2
6
1
8
7
5

2
3
4
2
8
9
6
5
7

NAMING THE WAVE

Pipeline, Pe'ahi (Jaws), Waimea. These are some of the most famous names in Hawai'i. In the world of surfing, the wave is a bigger star than any champion. Humans get old and fade away, but the waves keep rolling in. Famous surf break names aren't found only in Hawai'i. Mavericks in California, Manly in Australia, Cloudbreak in Fiji, and Teahupo'o in Tahiti are known to most surfers. Naming a surf break is a fundamental part of worldwide surfing culture, so much so that no one thinks twice about it. Every break has a personality, so naturally it has a name. But where did this tradition start?

Naming things is a deeply Hawaiian tradition. They name their houses, fish-hooks, surfboards, and canoes, but also mountains, streams, winds, and rains. Given the importance of surfing in Hawaiian culture, it's no surprise that naming their breaks is as old as surfing itself.

Waves come in all shapes and sizes, but it takes a very special kind of wave to be surfable. Those waves are born out of surf breaks—a complex combination of geography, geology, water, wind, flora, and fauna that gathers the ocean's energy and shapes it into a wave that we can ride.

What direction is the break facing? What's the shape of the ocean floor? Which way does the wind blow? Is there coral or kelp? No two surf breaks are the same. They are some of the most location-specific natural phenomena on the planet. Even a single stretch of beach can host many different surf breaks. Depending on conditions, Waikīkī Beach has almost a dozen surfable waves breaking at one time.

Wahi pana are culturally significant places celebrated in traditional Hawaiian genres. Surf breaks are one of those places. A surf break is a source of endless entertainment, athletic feats, and joy for a community. It is an object of constant study and storytelling. Surfers learn its behavior and quirks. It becomes their companion.

Oftentimes a break has its own legend to explain its history, but sometimes we can only guess why they earn names like Kamoa (the chicken) or Kamakai'a (the fish eye).

Some names are simply descriptions of the land where surf breaks are located: Hale-lua (pit house), Laupāhoehoe (smooth lava flat), Honokōhau (bay drawing dew). In other cases, names like Kahale'ula (the red house) or Niukūkahi (single coconut tree) might serve as reference points when surfers fix their location in the water by triangulating two landmarks. Sometimes the name describes the water: Kaipalaoa (whale sea), Kealakekua (moving current). Or the name can describe the wave itself: Waipi'o (curved water), Kalaloa (very rough), Pūhele (traveling hill). Some names are advice about who should ride it: 'Aiwohi (royal

NALU ALOHA O KA 'ĀINA HĀNAU.

Beloved waves of the birth land.

—'ŌLELO NO'EAU

Opposite, top: Aerial view of the reef that helps to form Pipeline surf break, North Shore, O'ahu

Opposite, bottom: The reef beneath Pipeline. Pipeline is so close to shore that it is usually only two to three feet deep. Surfers can collide with or get trapped in these reef crevices. This is one reason why Pipeline is one of the deadliest breaks in the world.

Following: Pipeline, North Shore, O'ahu

TALK STORY TOUR

KALEHUAWEHE

(WAIKĪKĪ, OʻAHU)

Pīkoiakaʻalalā is one of the great heroes of Hawaiian mythology. He was born into a family of rat shapeshifters. Perhaps that is why he was born with rat fur on his head instead of hair. Despite this, he was handsome and clever, with a supernatural talent for archery. He once shot and strung forty rats on a single arrow.

When Pīkoi was young, his family lived in Mānoa, Oʻahu. One day he wanted to wear a lehua lei while surfing, so he asked his sister to make one. She made two for his head and two for his neck. Thus adorned, Pīkoi went to Ulukou in Waikīkī—a break in front of where the Moana Hotel now stands. He saw Kahamaluʻihi, an aliʻi wahine (royal woman), riding a wave to shore. Pīkoi did not have a board, so he asked to use hers. She refused because her surfboard was kapu (prohibited); if anyone used it, she would have them killed.

Instead, she lent him her attendant's surfboard. As Pīkoi paddled off for the break called Kapuni, a local warned him to stay on one side because the other was reserved for Kahamaluʻihi. Neither was breaking, so Pīkoi paddled to Kaluaāhole, the next spot over, and Kahamaluʻihi followed him. After floating there for a bit, they decided to paddle to another spot, which didn't have a name because waves rarely broke there. Kahamaluʻihi found Pīkoi charming and admired his lei, so she asked him to give her one from his head. He untied the lei and retied them around her neck. This is how the break received the name Kalehuawehe—"the lehua [lei] that was untied."

In the late 1890s, missionary descendant J. B. Castle built a four-story home (now the site of the Elks Lodge) facing Kalehuawehe. Surfers renamed this break Castle's. Kalehuawehe breaks only in the summer, when swells exceed ten feet. As Duke Kahanamoku once famously demonstrated, it is possible to ride Kalehuawehe's swell all the way to Canoes, over a mile away.

Ma'alaea (modern name: Freight Train), Maui, 2024. This is an extremely rare wave, since it only begins truly firing when waves reach over twelve feet. The swell must come from a south/southwest swell in order to squeeze through the eight mile gap between the island of Kaho'olawe and the southwest tip of Maui, and also requires southeast winds to prevent it from crumbling. In the twenty-first century, Ma'alaea has only appeared three times: 2005, 2022, and 2024. When it does, surfers consider it the fastest wave in the world.

ruler) and Kalehua (the expert). One bay contains two surf breaks: Kaina (little brother, small waves close to shore) and Kua'ana (big brother, larger waves farther out in the bay).

By combing through legends, chants, old newspapers, and living memory, scholars can confirm and name some of the traditional surf sites used for centuries. The first definitive book on surfing, *Surfing* (1966) by Ben Finney and James D. Houston, lists 106 ancient Hawaiian surf breaks; however, the authors knew this was an undercount.

In 1996, researcher John Clark created a more complete map that showed the full extent of surfing in Hawaiian history when he counted around six hundred surfable waves—and the list is still growing. One reason for the increase is that modern equipment (smaller boards, kitesurfing, foil boarding, etc.) has opened previously unrideable surf breaks.

Another reason has to do with the terrible impact that Western contact has had upon Hawai'i. Hawai'i is estimated to have had a precontact population of almost one million people. By the early 1900s, epidemics from introduced diseases had reduced that population to forty thousand people. This demographic collapse caused an incalculable loss of knowledge. When foreign surfers explored the islands for waves, they gave new names to surf breaks. They replaced the existing culture with their own because of their desire to claim ownership and their lack of local knowledge. The naming of surf breaks over time tells a larger story of Hawaiian history.

When white business owners built their homes on the waterfront, these homes became the new landmarks. The surf break known as Kalehuawehe became Castle's.

During the plantation era, white landowners brought in workers from Asia. As these new arrivals took up residence in Hawai'i, their influence was felt in names like Fuji's, Kamisugi's, and Rice Bowl.

U.S. military buildup during World War II drastically altered the landscape. Waves that might once have been named after local stories or geography became Antennas, Gun Point, Marineland, Pillboxes, and Rifle Range. The military industrialized several harbors, but a little industrial waste wasn't going to stop surfers from chasing good waves. Ammonia is named for the smell that came off the heavy industrial tanks in Kaua'i's harbor. Crushers is just offshore from a gravel pit. Flies was named for the blackflies that swarm out from the local landfill to harass surfers and fishermen. Fumes gets covered in exhaust from the airport.

The rise of short boards in the 1960s and '70s enabled surfers to ride more waves, with many names reflecting the era's psychedelic vibe: Acid Drop, Bongs, Stone Zone, Pray for Sex.

Not every name bore the burden of marking history. Many Hawaiian traditions live on. For instance, the use of names as advice about who should ride a wave: Old Lady's, Rubber Duckies (for kids), and Turkey Bay (because only turkeys would ride it). Or a warning to those who dare to try: Tombstones, Point Panic, Insanities, Suicides, Terrors. Some of the names describe what the wave will do to you: Pounders, Razorblades (watch out for the coral), and Pinballs (you'll get bounced between the rocks if you're not careful).

Sometimes a surf break's name pinpoints its location, making it easier to find: Stone Shacks, White Fence, 68 (for the number on the utility pole marking where the wave breaks). But some surfers prefer to keep their favorite breaks hidden: No Can Tell, No Name, or just plain Secrets. Waves don't just arrive in certain places; some come only at certain times. Names can pass that information to the next generation: One wave is Consistents, while another is Blue Moon or even Olympics (because it seems to appear only every four years), and yet another is called Phantoms because, since it appears so seldom, it seems more legend than real.

Sometimes the only logic behind a name is a song or inside joke shared by friends when they discovered a wave, had a great day, and wanted to commemorate a particular moment. As long as these names exist, their stories live on. That is the closest we humans can come to matching the ageless wonder of a surf break and its endless supply of waves.

Marcus Biju at Gas Chambers,
Sandy's Beach, O'ahu

KA LEO O KE KAI
THE VOICE OF THE SEA

When we approach the ocean, we enter an amphitheater of sound. The music of the sea fills our senses. Hawaiians have listened to the ocean's ever-changing song for thousands of years. Here are some of their descriptions.

ROUGH SEA

Laolao: deep booming sound, as of distant surf
Kai olohia: resounding sea; a sea rough enough to produce sound
Kai leo nui: loud-voiced sea
Kai kōloa: roaring sea
Kai hāku'i: pounding sea that echoes
Kai halulu: thundering sea
Kai nākolo: rumbling sea, from huge breaking waves

Hawaiians memorialized the distinctive sound of the surf at certain locations in their traditional genres. Pukui notes, "There are numerous references in old Hawaiian poetry to the thunderous waves at Wai-a-lua being carried as far inland as Wahi-a-wā (place of noise)."

CALM SEA

Ke kuhō 'ana o ke kai: splashing of the sea
Kai 'owē / 'oē: murmuring sea
Kai nehe: rustling sea, as of waves washing over sand or pebbles
Kai hāwanawana: whispering sea

Avalanche in Waialua Bay, Hale'iwa

A EA MAI KE KAI O WAIALUA,
WAWĀ NŌ ʻŌLELO ʻOKOʻA I PALI,
NŪNŪ ME HE IHU NO KA PUAʻA HAE LA,
ʻAKO KA LAU O KA NALU PIʻI I KA PALI.

Let the sea of Wai-a-lua ascend,
let the echo carry into the hills
like the grunt of wild boar
while the wave, the climbing surf,
uproots seaside leaf from cliff.

—TRANS. BY MARY KAWENA PUKUI AND ALFONS L. KORN
FROM *THE ECHO OF OUR SONG*

ʻIKE KAI HOHONU

DEEP KNOWLEDGE OF THE SEA

To see people surfing and think, *I can do that, too,* requires confidence in your ocean abilities. To be the first person or people to look at waves thousands of years ago and think, *Those can be ridden,* requires ʻike kai hohonu—a deep knowledge of the sea.

Hawaiians have always been a water people. Their ancestors were seafaring as far back as 3,500 years ago. The ocean is in their DNA. As an islander, you begin to accumulate ʻike kai from birth. At first, this knowledge is sensory. You first experience the sea as a newborn in your parent's arms when they introduce you to Kanaloa and his cool, salty embrace. As a toddler dashing in and out of the waves that rush over the beach, you learn your first important lesson about the ocean: mai huli kou kua i ke kai—never turn your back on the sea.

Then you learn to swim, and your ʻike kai grows exponentially. You learn to hold your breath and experience the world below the surface.

You become subject to the ocean's laws. The first law is that it has a rhythm. At first the waves move you. Then you begin to move with the wave. You learn to ride the wave with your body, then with a board. You wipe out over and over and slowly realize that there is one special spot on a cresting wave that if you catch it just right, can slide you thrillingly fast and far toward the shore.

By the time you are old enough to hold a paddle, you are out on a canoe. You learn how to paddle and steer. The ocean becomes an open road that can take you out to the boundless expanse where it's only you, water, horizon, and sky. You will spend your entire life learning from the ocean and passing that ʻike kai on to the next generation.

KNOWLEDGE OF THE SEA LEADS TO EASE WITH THE SEA.

—MARIE ALOHALANI BROWN

MOVING IN THE OCEAN

When the first foreigners—mainly seamen—passed through the Hawaiian Islands between the late eighteenth and mid-nineteenth centuries, they marveled at the ease with which Hawaiians moved in the sea. Few European sailors could swim, and those who could were barely proficient. Captain James Cook, who chanced upon the Hawaiian Islands in 1778, offers the first known commentary: "[The people of Kaua'i] are vigorous, active, and most expert swimmers; leaving their canoes upon the most trifling occasion; diving under them, and swimming to others though at a great distance. It was very common to see women, with infants at the breast, when the surf was so high that they could not land in the canoes, leap overboard, and without endangering their little ones, swim to the shore, through a sea that looked dreadful."

I HARDLY REMEMBER WHETHER I LEARNED HOW TO WALK OR HOW TO SWIM FIRST.

—DUKE KAHANAMOKU

In 1836, French diplomat Théodore-Adolphe Barrot watched Hawaiian women swimming in Kealakekua Bay on Hawai'i Island:

> Towards noon, the entire female population of Kealakeakua assembled to bathe in a small bay surrounded by lava rocks; one rock served the bathers for a screen, and they plunged thence entirely naked, into the waves which were breaking upon the shore; a plank, six or eight feet in length, and pointed at one end, enabled them to sustain themselves on the crest of the waves. It was indeed, a singular picture—a swarm of young women

Captain James Cook's arrival to Kealakeua Bay, Hawai'i Island in 1778. The man on the board (lower left) is the earliest known Western depiction of a surfboard.

passing far out to sea, then returning with the swiftness of an arrow, borne upon the foaming crests of the surges which break with the noise of thunder on each side of the bay. I expected every moment to see them dashed against sharp points of the rocks, but they avoided the danger with surprising address; indeed, danger seemed to delight them, and they dared to defy it with a courage which astonished me. The least movement of their body gave to the plank which sustained them, the desired direction, and disappearing for a moment in the midst of the breakers, they very soon arose from the foam and returned at their ease to run the same race again. I saw a mother, who having placed her child, scarcely a year old, upon a plank two feet long, pushed it before her to a great distance, and then abandoning it to the fury of the waves, she followed, directing only now and then the plank which sustained it. . . .

The next day I spoke to Mr. Forbes concerning the extraordinary dexterity in swimming which I had observed on the preceding day among the natives. "You can have no adequate idea of it," he replied, "they are more at their ease in the water than on land."

While outside observers marveled at Hawaiians' expertise in the water, for Hawaiians themselves, this was simply a part of their culture. Their mythology and lives were filled with stories that celebrated and normalized incredible feats of ocean-ability. We can see this in the many tales of channel crossings.

[*Frontispiece.*

Maui, 1873

MAI HULI KOU KUA I KE KAI.

NEVER TURN YOUR BACK ON THE SEA.

For generations, parents have warned their children, "Mai huli kou kua i ke kai."

Like all good advice, it works on many levels. On a practical level, if you don't pay attention, you can die. On a more profound level, it is meant to instill a deep respect for the ocean. When you are near the ocean, you are in the presence of the greatest power on earth. Most importantly, this warning teaches you the ocean's defining trait: The ocean is always changing.

It requires you to be present, aware, and willing to adapt. A calm sea can start to rage. A raging sea can become serene. The ocean can birth a new beach overnight or swallow one whole. Waves that are bigger than usual can arrive without warning. In Hawai'i alone, these "sneaker waves" drag dozens to their deaths every year. So listen to your elders!

Nine channels separate the eight main islands. Hawaiians knew these channels well because they traveled them frequently in canoes. These can be inhospitable places, long distances filled with powerful currents, high winds, huge swells, and plenty of sharks. When someone decided to make the journey solo, it became the stuff of legend.

Kaikipa'ananea, who ruled Kaua'i sometime during the thirteenth century, traveled solo on a surfboard across the treacherous thirty-mile-wide 'Alenuihāhā Channel that separates Maui and Hawai'i. Tom "Pōhaku" Stone (see "The Art of Shaping Boards," page 93), who made this same solo journey in 1987, explains that the strong winds in this channel can whip up waves as high as forty feet. The eighteen-to-twenty-foot olo surfboard, which Kaikipa'ananea was most likely using, allows the rider to catch giant waves that do not break, so he could alternate between paddling and surfing.

In the sixteenth century, Kihapi'ilani, ruler of Maui, decided to accompany several ali'i on their trip to Molokai. While they took a canoe, he paddled his olo. He was the first person to paddle the eight miles across the windswept, choppy sea of the Pailolo Channel. Legend has it that the waves did not wet his lei until he landed ashore.

The most incredible swimming feat belongs to Hainakolo, a beloved but tragic heroine. She lived north of Ni'ihau on the mythical island of Kuaihelani with her husband and child. When her husband abandoned her for her sister, her grief overwhelmed her judgment. With her young son's arms around her neck, she swam the length of the island chain back to her birthplace on Hawai'i Island, around two hundred nautical miles. As her strength waned, two akua who embody ocean currents, Keaumiki and Keaukā, took pity on her and helped her complete the journey.

In Hawai'i, the line between legend and reality can be blurry. There are so many true stories of Hawaiian swimming prowess that one newspaper dedicated a column to these feats. All the following events took place in the open ocean off the island of Molokai in the early 1900s.

One story tells of a Hawaiian French fisherman whose boat overturned, but he survived by swimming for seventeen hours straight. He might have gone quicker, but he was light-skinned and did not remove his trousers for fear that his white legs would attract sharks (a Hawaiian belief).

Opposite: Lāna'i at dawn

Below: This column appeared in dozens of newspapers across the United States. It coincided with Duke Kahanamoku's record-breaking appearance at the 1912 Olympics and the American fascination with all things Hawaiian.

His bare chest certainly attracted attention. Upon reaching shore, he discovered that spiny crabs had clamped onto his torso.

In 1911, a fishing boat with a crew of eight men went down at sea. The captain, Sam Manu, was Hawaiian, while the other seven were Koreans. Manu was the lone survivor. Just after he shed his clothes to make swimming more manageable, something bumped him. In true Hawaiian storytelling fashion, Manu managed to turn a tragic account into a humorous tale:

> I had never been afraid of sharks. I have swum and dived and played with sharks, like other Hawaiians, but when I felt that thing bump into me I think my heart stopped beating. I didn't mind being drowned not so much, because my boat was gone, and I was old, but I didn't want my old body torn to pieces to make kaukau (food) for sharks.
>
> But it wasn't a shark that hit me. It was just a good friendly piece of board, as I found out when I hit out against it, determined to make a fight for my life. I ought to have known that a shark wouldn't have come smelling me that way. I stuck the board under my arm and floated a bit more till I found another—a two by four piece about four feet long . . . and I crossed them into an X, put my arms over them and struck out with my legs.
>
> Molokai was about 25 miles away. Lanai, the next nearest island, was a little further, but the wind was offshore from Molokai, and I decided to make Lanai my port. The wind and current helped me and the stars wheeling their way across the sky told me my course and measured off the hours for me. When the gray morning came it found me strong, feeling well and rid of all the nervousness and excitement. By treading water when the waves lifted me up, I could see the hills of Lanai red in the rising sun.
>
> That was something to encourage me and I got back to my swimming.
>
> All that morning I swam, and I had lots of time to think. . . . I went over all my wrecks as I kicked along and watched Lanai rising higher and higher out of the water.
>
> It was about noon when I dragged myself up the rocks at Kaena Point. I had been in the water since half-past eight o'clock the night before, and I am 77 years old.

These people are truly amphibious. . . .
The children riot in the waves from their infancy. . . .
I saw great fat men with their hair streaked with grey . . .
riding the surges shoreward with as much
enjoyment as if they were in their first youth.

—ISABELLA BIRD, EXPLORER AND WRITER, HILO, HAWAIʻI (1872)

This third story shows, happily, that not all mishaps at sea end in tragedy. In 1912, a Sunday-school party set off on a schooner for an excursion along the coast. The group consisted of several adults and numerous children, including "a dozen or so" who were "not more than three years old." Two miles offshore, a sudden gust overturned the boat and dumped them in the water. Instead of panicking, they "paddled gaily back to land." Not a single person was injured.

THE ART OF READING LAND, SEA, AND SKY

Surfing is an activity that requires intense observation. How are the waves breaking? Where and in what shape? How many are in a set? What is the tide like, and where is the wind coming from? But that's not enough. The ocean is forever changing, so waves can change within minutes.

Pe'ahi earned the nickname Jaws in 1975 when three surfers saw ten-foot waves. But by the time they paddled out to the break, the waves had morphed into twenty-foot-plus monsters that raked them over the famously rocky shore. They escaped, requiring a few stitches but gaining a new piece of knowledge—that particular surf break can bite you hard. In the ocean, you need to know both what is and also what will be.

It is no coincidence that the culture that created and mastered he'e nalu is the same culture that spawned master navigators. Polynesian voyagers crossed the Pacific using nothing but their powers of observation combined with many generations' worth of collective memory. They used celestial bodies (stars, constellations, and the moon), winds and clouds, currents, swells, the ocean's color, seabirds, and fish to chart their route, predict the weather, and guide them safely—even when they were heading to places they'd never been.

It's safe to say most surfers are not experts at Polynesian wayfinding. There are around thirty million surfers worldwide and only a handful of master navigators. But both activities draw from the same deep well of knowledge. What follows is a small sample of that 'ike kai.

Opposite: Ho'okipa, Maui

Pe'ahi (modern name: Jaws), Maui, on a calm day

Pe'ahi firing. The wave itself travels at approximately twenty miles per hour, and surfers like Kai Lenny (pictured) can reach speeds of fifty miles per hour at the bottom of the slope.

READING THE LAND AND SEA

A red pawa (predawn) sky announces that good waves will soon arrive.

Hawaiians were masters of observing the minute variations in natural phenomena. They recorded over three hundred rains, six hundred winds, dozens of clouds, and over ten kinds of rainbows. They gave these phenomena descriptive and often poetic names and memorialized them—and did the same for the ocean.

Ocean and land are intimately connected and continuously influence each other. The land's features affect how the ocean behaves. For instance, the beach with the highest rate of spinal injuries is not the famously dangerous reef break of Pipeline. It's the shore break of Wāwāmalu (also known as Sandy Beach). Its sandy bottom creates waves that barrel in shallow water (one to three feet). Experienced bodyboarders and bodysurfers love it, but because the wave breaks right on shore, it attracts casual beachgoers as well . . . who get drilled into the ground. Wāwāmalu is equally famous for ripping off women's bathing suits. A retired lifeguard confessed that the best part of his job was when women pressed against him to shield themselves as he helped them out of the water.

Hawaiians identified twenty-five separate zones in the ocean from where the sea rushes inland to where the ocean seemingly ends at the horizon. Many of these zones reflect the interaction of land and sea, and how humans interact in them.

THE OCEAN'S ZONES

Coastal areas: ʻAe kai is where the sea breaks and rushes inland. Poʻeana kai and puʻe are just past ʻae kai, but do not apply to reefs. Where people wade is kai heleku and kai pāpaʻu. Kuaʻau is a reef covered by water that is shallow enough for people to stand in but deep enough to swim over. A kuaʻau marks where the shallows ends and the deep sea begins.

Open ocean: Next are kai au (swimming sea), hohonu (deep sea), kai ʻōkilo heʻe (where octopuses are caught using the ʻōkilo method), kai heʻe nalu (sea for surfing; a surf break that is farther out, like Populars in Waikīkī), kohola (outer reef), kai uli (dark blue sea), kai lūheʻe (where octopuses are caught using cowry lures), kai mālolo (where flying fish are found), and kai ʻōpelu (where mackerel are found). Then kai hī aku (where fishermen troll for aku or skipjack tuna), kai koholā (where whales are found), and kai kakaka (where deep-sea fishing is done).

Deep ocean: Moana (open ocean) is the deepest part of the sea, also called waha lilo (far outside), kai lewa (deep sea out of sight of land), and lipo (deep blue-black). The moana extends to kahikimoe (the horizon), the last zone.

ʻEʻEHIA: EERIE

ʻEʻehia describes a person or place that makes you uneasy. When a place is ʻeʻehia, perhaps it was the site of a great battle or terrible event. It is wise to avoid such areas, no matter how tempting they may be. Over generations of interaction with the ocean, we build a collective memory of where bad things are more likely to happen (such as encounters with sharks, riptides, or powerful currents). These collective memories impart valuable lessons, especially when today's surfers are hungry to boost their reputation and social media engagement by searching for ever more exotic and high-risk locales. As Hawaiians say, listen to your naʻau—your gut instinct. ʻEʻehia reminds us that nature can kill you.

Sandy's Beach, Oʻahu

READING THE SKY

The art of reading clouds (and other signs) is termed *ha'i 'ōuli*. A seer who uses clouds to divine the future is called a *nānā ao*. Cloud names are based on the kind of weather they announce and their resemblance to other things in the island world. Clouds are more than just natural phenomena. They can be gods. Uakoko, rainbow-colored clouds, are Kāne. Lono embodies the dark storm clouds of the winter season. Ao 'īlio (dog clouds) are Kū. Pua'a (pig clouds), banks of fog or puffy clouds, are the forms of the demigod Kamapua'a (pig child). 'Ena is an opening in the clouds likened to the jaws of the a'u (swordfish), a sign of rain.

Hawaiians also heed the color of the sky. Aka'ula, when the lower part of the western evening sky is red, means the rain will soon clear. Pāuli, when that same area of sky is dark, means the sea is about to become rough.

'IKE MAKANI: WIND KNOWLEDGE

Makani is the general term for wind, and clouds are poetically referred to as nā maka o ka makani (eyes of the wind) because they are closely connected. 'Ike makani can save your life at sea. Pius "Mau" Piailug, the master navigator who trained the first modern generation of Hawaiian navigators, maintained: "If you want to find the first sign of a weather change, look high."

There are seasonal winds and place-specific winds. Every district on every island has one or more famous winds. In Kaua'i, there are three makani he'e nalu (surfing winds) that create good surf conditions: Hauola shapes the surf at Wailua Bay, Ho'olua for Makaiwa, near Wailua, and Kolokini at Hā'ena.

Hawaiians talk to the winds. In one legend, a descendant of a wind goddess used his wind mana to summon large waves to kill his enemies:

Eia ho'i au o ka make!
A make 'oe o ka 'ale iki,
A make 'oe o ka 'ale nui
A make 'oe o ka 'ale loa,
A make 'oe o ka 'ale poko,
He 'ale po'i no ka wa'a hemahema
Kau a akamai 'ole o ka ho'okele

Here I am to destroy you!
The small wave will destroy you,
The large wave will destroy you,
The long wave will destroy you,
The short wave will destroy you,
A wave crashing down on the unprepared canoe
Shows that the steersmen are unskillful.

ʻIKE AO

Dr. Kalei Nuʻuhiwa is a Hawaiian scholar-practitioner from Maui.

She lectures worldwide about her groundbreaking research on traditional knowledge, including Hawaiian practices of celestial timekeeping, rituals, and ceremonies. Her expertise is Papahulilani, the study of heavenly cycles and atmospheric phenomena. Here she offers two examples.

"Ao nuʻa look like rolling waves in the sky. They typically form when storms pass Hawaiʻi and predict the arrival of good surf waves in the next day or two."

"Ao ʻīlio run in packs like dogs from one side of the sky to the other. They announce a change in weather, good or bad."

TALKING TO THE OCEAN

The ocean is a living thing, aware and capable of having feelings. For Hawaiians, this sentience exists in all nature, so naturally they and their heroes talked to the ocean. When the sea was flat and people wanted to surf, they called to the ocean to bring up waves.

The most common ritual was to take a length of pōhuehue, a beach morning-glory vine that grows on the shoreline, then whip it around your head and strike it against the water while chanting to the sea. Many begin with the command "Kū mai, kū mai ka nalu!" (Rise, let the wave rise!). One chant likens swells to gourds, a common metaphor in Hawaiian poetics because both are big and round:

Hō aʻe, hō aʻe i luna i ka pōhuehue,
Ka ipu nui lawe mai,
Ka ipu iki waiho aku.

Rise up, let the pōhuehue cause you to rise high.
Bring forth the great gourd,
Set aside the small gourd.

You can also perform this ritual when you are already surfing. In one legend, three boys needed a large wave to carry them to shore. One boy asked the ocean to bring the perfect wave:

Kū mai,
Kū mai ka nalu nui
Mai Kahiki mai,
Popoʻi kaiuli kai ea,
Kai piʻi i ka pōhuehue
I ka lau mahiki,
Apo aku apo mai,
Kai apo ʻāpuni,
Kai apo,
A lawa a koe koena,
I ke alo o Hoʻomiha la e pā

Rise,
Let the great wave rise
From Tahiti,
Let the deep dark blue sea rise and break with a roar,
Let the sea rise because of the pōhuehue
Because of the leaf tips
Circling around
A noisy, brawling high tide
A high tide
Let it be so ample that the excess
Reaches and touches Hoʻomiha.

When he finished, a huge swell rose in the distance like a mountain. The three friends caught the wave and flew across its face like the wind, all the way to shore.

While calling up waves is not as widespread as it once was, some families still practice this tradition and pass it on to their children.

Opposite: Darrick Doerner, Outside Sunset, Oʻahu

Following: Ritualist Lanakila Mangauil at the opening ceremonies for the 2023 Da Hui Backdoor Shootout, North Shore, Oʻahu

ME'E NO HE'E NALU: Surfing Hero

HI'IAKAIKAPOLIOPELE

Many gods surf in Hawaiian mythology, but by far the most prolific and greatest of all time was Hi'iakaikapoliopele. Hi'iaka is the ultimate water-woman. She is a big-wave rider, wave-summoner, surf reporter, lifeguard, master canoe paddler, and water-healer.

Hi'iaka began life as an egg on the idyllic island of Bora Bora. She was immediately thrust into the intense drama of the Pele clan. After a family dispute, Hi'iaka, Pele, and most of their siblings fled in a canoe to escape the wrath of their eldest sister, Nāmakaokaha'i, who tried to kill them with a tsunami.

After they reached the island of Hawai'i and settled down, Pele and her sisters decided to spend a day on the beach of Nanahuki at Kea'au.

There they saw a beautiful woman named Hōpoe dancing on the shore. She taught Hi'iaka how to hula, to use her body to imitate the rhythms and motion of nature.

Then Hōpoe took her out on the water and taught her how to he'e nalu, to use her body and board to imitate the rhythms and motion of the sea. Hi'iaka was hooked. She became a master waterwoman. Her favorite waves were giants from the deep. She split her time between surfing and attending to the (many) needs of her dramatic sister.

One day, Pele wanted to see her newest lover, a Kaua'i ali'i named Lohi'au, so she sent Hi'iaka to fetch him. This was a dangerous journey and Hi'iaka was a young goddess who had yet to come into her powers, so Pele bestowed on her two gifts: a fern skirt imbued with the power of lightning that also doubled as a surfboard, and Kīlauea, a supernatural hand that Hi'iaka could command to perform tasks like traveling great distances to fetch seawater or pluck surfers out of the jaws of sharks. Hi'iaka then embarked on an epic journey (the translation is almost 450 pages long). She traveled from island to island, battling hostile humans and supernatural beings. The epic of Hi'iaka is also the world's very first surf tour. It acted as a compendium of surf legends from Hawai'i's earliest days. She surfed with ali'i, playing with some and punishing others. She saw an entire village of ghosts—men, women, and children—surfing. She met a mo'o god who surfed the thundering waves of Waimea Bay.

MY WAVE THAT I SURF IN THE SEA OF MY LAND IS THE LONG-BACKED SWELL OF THE DEEP DARK-BLUE OCEAN. WHEN THE SEA RISES AND ALMOST CONCEALS THE MOUNTAIN OF [MAUNA] KEA, THEN MY WAVE HAS ARRIVED.

—HI'IAKAIKAPOLIOPELE

Her greatest triumph came when she finally found Lohi'au, only to discover that two mo'o goddesses had killed him and trapped his soul. She rescued his soul and reunited it with his body. But she couldn't bring Pele a boyfriend who reeked of death, so she asked the gods to send her towering waves. Then she took Lohi'au out in the water and surfed him back to health.

The return voyage didn't go quite as well. Hi'iaka returned to find that Pele had killed Hōpoe. Out of spite, Hi'iaka seduced Lohi'au. Now, *lohi'au* means *slow*, and while Lohi'au was famously good-looking, he wasn't very bright, which is possibly why he had sex with Hi'iaka on the edge of Kīlauea Crater in front of Pele and her family. Pele made her feelings known by burning him to death.

Hi'iaka went back to her regular life—hanging with her sisters, dancing hula, and surfing. No one has reported sightings of her in human form in recent years, but she is immortal. When the waves are gigantic, you can be sure she is still out there riding.

A CHIEFESS IGNORES HI'IAKA'S WARNING

(HILO, HAWAI'I)

On Hiʻiakaikapoliopele's travels around the islands, she and her traveling companion, Wahineʻōmaʻo, came to Punahoa, a beach in Hilo named after a beautiful chiefess who loved to surf there. Hiʻiaka enjoyed watching talented surfers, so they stopped when they saw a crowd admiring Punahoa as she glided back and forth across waves, surfing their curls.

The people likened her elegant stance to the beauty of an ʻiwa bird gliding in the wind. As the chiefess mounted yet another wave, a rainbow appeared directly above her.

Hiʻiaka and Wahineʻōmaʻo overheard several women and men arguing loudly about Punahoa's surfing. The women admired her surfing, whereas the men belittled her skills. The women found the men obnoxious and began to argue.

Wahineʻōmaʻo asked Hiʻiaka, "Who do you think is right?"

"Skilled surfers don't let a wave take control of their boards," said Hiʻiaka. "If the chiefess isn't more careful, she risks losing control of her board."

A woman overheard Hiʻiaka and ran to tell the others. Offended, one woman asked her to point out this stranger. When the group turned to look, they were taken aback. They had not expected the strangers to be so attractive, and while both women were stunning, Hiʻiaka was the perfect embodiment of Hawaiian beauty. The rosy glow of her cheeks with her golden-brown skin and the enticing curves of her body brought to mind a delectable feast served in a finely carved wooden bowl.

Once Punahoa came to shore, the villagers told her what Hiʻiaka said. Punahoa took offense and ordered her servants to fetch them. When Punahoa saw how beautiful Hiʻiaka was, she grew even angrier and challenged Hiʻiaka to a surfing contest. If Hiʻiaka lost, she would pay the price with her bones (she would be killed).

Hiʻiaka calmly replied, "There is no need for a challenge. If you don't lose your board, my bones will be yours, but I have seen what will pass. The current has changed and now heads toward Kumukahi Point, and now the sets have also changed. A surfer will see the first wave and think it's worth catching, but they'd be wrong because these sets will be crowded, and the current will cause the steep curl to collapse. That is when the wave will take control of the board and drag the surfer down. Before the surfer can surface, another wave will drag them across the coral reef. This is why I urge you not to risk your life by going out."

As Punahoa walked away, Hiʻiaka called out one last warning: "Do not do this. I have also foreseen that when you catch a wave, a shark will ride it with you, and I will be the one to save you. My companion and I will leave this place only once we have seen that your board has broken."

Punahoa ignored Hiʻiaka and paddled out to her favorite spot, just as Hiʻiaka had predicted, the sea changed. Everyone noticed that the waves were now behaving oddly, as if they were fighting each other.

When a massive wave loomed, Punahoa went for it. As she mounted the swell, everyone was horrified to see the dorsal fin of a huge shark emerge right behind her. Then, just as Hiʻiaka foresaw, the wave closed out. Punahoa lost control of her board and fell headfirst into the sea, with the shark right behind her.

Before Punahoa could resurface, a second wave broke and was about to drag her body across the coral reef, when Hiʻiaka thrust out her hand of power, Kīlauea. It shot through the sea like a torpedo, grabbed Punahoa by the thigh, and dragged her back to shore, her body skipping over the water's surface like a stone.

Kīlauea placed the battered Punahoa on the sand, then plunged back into the rough sea to deal with the shark. The supernatural hand sped through the ocean and slammed into the shark so hard that it flew out of the water.

The crowd saw the water explode. The shark's body flew up into the air, landed with a crash at their feet, and then turned to stone. The stone shark was half in and half out of the water and looked like an ordinary boulder on the shore. (That's where it has remained ever since, but don't look for it now, because sand has long since covered it.)

One of the villagers picked up the broken remnants of Punahoa's surfboard and placed them at her feet as she lay on the beach, unable to speak and exhausted by her ordeal. This was a fate she could easily have avoided if she had been humble enough to listen to those wiser in the ways of the ocean.

Then Hiʻiaka and Wahineʻōmaʻo, true to their word, left that place and traveled on.

Rosie Jaffurs

Laird Hamilton

LOCAL MANNERS

While disguised as a human, Hi'iaka passed through O'ahu and stopped to watch an ali'i named Palani surfing his local break of Kahana. She was so impressed with his skills that she sang a chant of praise for him. The arrogant Palani had no idea who she was and berated her for daring to speak his name. Hi'iaka decided to teach him a lesson, so she called to the sea:

Kū mai! Kū mai ka nalu!
Popo'i kai uli, kai ko'o,
Iwi ko'o i ke kai, 'ō 'ia ka papa
'O Palani, 'o ke ali'i he'enalu o Kahana
'O Palani—'oe—
'Ō—ia!

Rise! Let the waves rise!
Let the deep sea rise and break with a roar, a rough sea
Let a long line of rough waves appear in the sea, the board will tumble.
Palani, the surfing ali'i of Kahana
Palani—you—
Will—be thrust down!

Out of nowhere, a gigantic wave rose up and crashed down upon Palani, dragging him to his death. Old-timers of Kahana say that a certain stone at that break is his corpse. Let this be a lesson to all who surf their local spots. Be gracious to enthusiastic outsiders, for you never know—they might be a god in disguise.

PART 2

HE‘E NALU

WAVE SLIDING

How would you like to stand like a god before the crest of a monster billow, always rushing to the bottom of a hill and never reaching its base, and to come rushing in for half a mile at express speed, in graceful attitude, of course, until you reach the beach and step easily from the wave to the strand?

—DUKE KAHANAMOKU (1911)

Brian Keaulana at Pe'ahi

THE ART OF SHAPING BOARDS

A CONVERSATION WITH TOM "PŌHAKU" STONE

When the first person to hand you a surfboard and push you out into the water is Duke Kahanamoku, surfing is your destiny. Not only did Tom "Pōhaku" Stone become one of the best surfers of his generation, he is one of the most influential board makers alive. In the 1970s, Pōhaku surfed Pipeline, competed professionally, and appeared on magazines and in surf movies. But that life never sat quite right with him: "I entered my first competition when I was fifteen. I got halfway through and then I just left. It just wasn't for me. That's not what surfing's about."

Turning away from competitive surfing didn't mean leaving the ocean behind. He became one of the legendary North Shore lifeguards, saving dozens of people every day. In his spare time, he squeezed in some extraordinary feats of oceangoing. In 1987, he became the first person to windsurf every channel of Hawai'i. He paddled a canoe the entire length of the eight main Hawaiian islands and made multiple solo channel crossings by paddleboard.

Pōhaku's interest in traditional Hawaiian sports brought him to Kapi'olani Community College, where his research single-handedly revived the ancient extreme sport of hōlua sledding (page 95). He then dedicated the rest of his life to shaping and surfing traditional wooden boards.

When he taught at Kapi'olani Community College, coauthor Alohalani, who was his student, was grateful that when the surf was up, Pōhaku would cancel class. She fondly remembers surfing with him those days and the epic camp-out at Mālaekahana when the class tried out the wooden boards they made. Pōhaku has mentored many of today's wooden board makers. His mission is to reestablish the philosophical and spiritual connection that exists between nature and board maker, the wood and the wave.

BACK TO THE BEGINNING (IN PŌHAKU'S OWN WORDS)

I grew up at the end of an era and the beginning of another one.

The first surfboards that I rode were all wood. But I discarded them. My cousin had the modern foam surfboards, and I wanted to know about those. In the process, I forgot what my beginnings really were. As time went on, I realized that I was not going anywhere with my surfing. Something was missing, and that missing part was knowing about that past and being able to understand it. That's what it's really about—relearning something that I was discarding that was so important to my surfing, the beginning of it. What brought me into surfing and my love for it and my desire to keep surfing, how I connect to the ocean.

That's what brings me full circle. I needed to go back to the past to improve my surfing abilities. Everyone was saying how great surfers are today, but in reality, our kūpuna were the true experts. To be able to ride a board like that in varying conditions of waves and sizes was just phenomenal. People have no damn idea today, but I do. It's our story.

I understood that you didn't need all this modernization of the surfboard. Yes, there's some maneuvers you can't do. But it allowed me to understand wood, and how crafting it was important because the functionality depended on how the dimensions were put into a particular wood and board that you wanted to ride. Because every one of them is different. The only thing that remains really the same is the glide. With wood boards, you're in harmony with the wave, and the modernized way is you're trying to dominate the wave. It's two different things.

I started making wooden boards because spiritually it made me feel connected to our kūpuna. I wasn't just making them, I was experiencing what I grew up with as a kid—what the hell my family, my uncles were trying to teach me. I just needed to know more and remember more. I was just continually moving forward to establish the narrative of our traditional practices that I was immersed in my entire life.

HE'E HŌLUA: SLED RIDING

While not traditionally included in books on surfing history, some scholar-practitioners believe that Hawaiian sled riding may be the origin of surfing itself. Whether this is true or not, he'e hōlua speaks to the ancient Hawaiians' love of finding insane ways to travel at great speeds (up to 50 mph!). While no one can say how hōlua sliding came to be, we can surmise how it began. Koa forests grow in the uplands, so harvesting trees requires working on steep slopes. Hawaiians guided the trees with ropes down through the forest, scraping a pathway. At some point, an adventurous soul tried sliding down one of those pathways on a log or plank. Soon they built sleds and runways on the rocky slopes of volcanoes for the sole purpose of sliding. Like surfing, he'e hōlua became an integral part of the culture—performed at festivals and religious ceremonies, and as a way for royalty and warriors to test their courage. It also has the highest level of celebrity endorsement—he'e hōlua is one of Pele's favorite hobbies.

THE OCEAN IS OUR LIFE, OUR MANA, OUR ‘OHANA.

—TOM “PŌHAKU” STONE

MANA AND THE MAKER (IN PŌHAKU'S OWN WORDS)

Whenever I start to work on a new piece of wood, I'm totally aware of using my mana as I shape it. All the way. Everything that I work with is reclaimed wood—what people don't want. But even that is important because every single piece of wood I work with has a spirit.

Everything is living. It's just that people don't see it that way today. The effort I put in is to try and connect with that life, which is the most important thing before I can do anything. Sometimes it takes a long time. It's being able to allow the pain and suffering that this individual life force is going through, and to say to it that together, there's new life. There's always a way. I don't like dry wood. It's hard to work with because dry means the wood is close to death. I don't want it to lose the life force that's in it. People go, "Oh no, it's got to be cured." I go, "Please don't." Saltwater gives us life. Life all comes from saltwater. So we keep applying saltwater to the wood.

Sometimes if the planks of wood don't want to transform and regain their rebirth as boards—their new life in a new form—you can't do anything about it. Some of the boards I made took five years. I think that's the longest I ever had. It took many dreams, and finally, we connected.

The answer is in dreams in which I've gone on a journey with one of my kūpuna, then when I wake in the mornings and tell my wife [Anne], "Oh, I know how to do this." I'm a spirit walker. I'm a dream walker. It's in our DNA. You're talking about thousands of years of DNA, and it's the guidance of our kūpuna in that moment, in our most aware state, when we are not part of this physical reality around us that allows us to walk back there and to be part of it. That's what happens to me. It's an opportunity to go back to where we actually come from. It's hard for people outside to understand that. But it is the reality. It's the only way.

We live in a world that's disconnected from the actual spirit of ka honua, our mother earth. People don't believe in the symbiotic relationship that we have. But I do. For the surfboard to become what it's going to become, it must be able to speak to me. I don't do anything that it doesn't want. I just follow the calling of that spirit. And every night, if I'm working with that individual entity, I listen to it. I hear it. And the next day, I know what it wants, and I just do it.

As a people, when we did something that involved our kūpuna, we did it with their approval—and we still do. Then the board has a living life again. You were just one small part of maintaining that spirit. That was so important to us not only culturally, not only in traditional practices, but to us staying in harmony with who we are, with everything around us. That's what's important to me. It's not about the money. It's not about "it's pretty." That's why it's hard to work with people who don't get it. It's about this individual that's taken form and a new life.

TRADITIONAL BOARDS OF HAWAI'I

BY PŌHAKU AND ANNE STONE

The husband-and-wife team of Pōhaku and Anne Stone have been working, researching, and riding traditional boards for decades. Their goal is to revive the lost knowledge of ancient Hawaiian surfers but also to provide a new path forward for future generations to explore. Their knowledge of the vast array of traditional boards is unparalleled, thus making them the perfect guides for this board tour. Here are the Stones' explanation of each board type.

❶ **Uma.** Believed to be the original surfboard that came from the Central Pacific with our Polynesians ancestors to Hawai'i, the uma is a small board used primarily for bodyboarding. During Captain Cook's first voyage to Tahiti in 1769, naturalist Joseph Banks described this style of board as resembling the "stern [back] of a broken canoe," which he witnessed Tahitians using to ride waves to shore with much speed and skill. *Uma* has multiple meanings, including "canoe stern," and *umauma* means "chest." Traditionally, surfers used this board to catch a wave and then pulled it underneath their chests. This allowed them to raise their arms, so they resembled the outstretched wings of a bird, such as the mōlī (albatross), gliding across the face of a wave. As one of the earliest board types, the uma provided the template for larger Hawaiian surfboards, and like all boards, they were made to fit the individual surfer.

❷ **'Ōwili.** The 'ōwili is another one of the smaller traditional Hawaiian surfboards. The name *'ōwili* may reference wiliwili, the type of wood used to make these lightweight boards as well as the coiling (barreling) of a wave. Surfers ride 'ōwili like they do the uma, but due to its larger size, more of the board would be beneath the surfer's body, which requires more skill to keep the board from nose-diving.

❸ **Paha.** The paha was common because it was easily made from wood left over from other projects, like what is carved out of the interior of a canoe. Children can easily ride this type of board, as it is the ideal choice to use in waves breaking near the shore. Usually ridden as a bodyboard, the paha is easy to maneuver in the surf, making for an exciting ride. It is also the forerunner to the more modern paipo board that Waikīkī beach boys used to teach tourists to surf in the 1920s.

❹ **Omo.** The omo represents an important transition in traditional surfboard designs, when Hawaiians made the leap from riding waves in a prone position to standing upright. The omo's length and its wider square tail allowed for the innovation of standing, but it was still small enough to be used prone. Beginning in the 1800s, board makers often used redwood to make these boards. Many early photos of surfing in Waikīkī feature omo boards.

❺ **ʻŌnini.** The ʻōnini style surfboard officially set the stage for surfing as we know it today. No longer were surfers lying prone and surfing across the face of the wave. Instead, they were crouching or standing on their boards, allowing them to develop new techniques and surfing reef breaks and farther away from shore.

This surfboard design is narrower in comparison to the omo and thus easier to maneuver through the curl of the wave. Most Hawaiian children learned to surf waves on an ʻōnini in a standing position before moving on to larger surfboards such as the kīkoʻo, puʻua, and olo, which are much more difficult to use.

❻ **Alaiʻa.** The alaiʻa was the most common board design in the past and is one of the more well-known boards in the present. *Alaiʻa* means "the path of the fish." The thin board flexes and turns like a fish in response to the pressure of the surfer's weight and the wave. Due to its speed and performance, the alaiʻa allows the rider to easily maneuver the surfboard across a wave. This makes it a popular choice even today for anyone who experiments with this traditional technology and combines it with a modern surfing mindset.

❼ **Kīoe.** Expert surfers of old probably favored the kīoe. It is a challenging surfboard to ride, thinner and narrower than many of the previously mentioned styles. Surfers used this board to ride a steep wave face in a standing, kneeling, or prone position. In the standing position, riders used their hands and/or feet to control their speed and influence the board's direction, enabling the surfer to stay near the curl of the wave. In 1937, John Kelly combined and modified the traditional surfboard shapes of the kīoe and kīkoʻo to create the Hot Curl—a breakthrough in modern surfboard design.

❽ **Puʻua.** The puʻua is a relatively unknown board, like the alaiʻa but more difficult to surf. Its unique design, with a wide nose and a pulled-in tail, gives it a teardrop shape. This board has a subtle convex top and bottom that requires the surfer to have good balance, but it gives the rider the ability to get this board into trim on the face of a wave, allowing it to have maximum glide.

❾ **Kīkoʻo.** When people think of surfing at the beginning of the twentieth century, they think of photos of Duke Kahanamoku and early Waikīkī beach boys. The boards in those images are most closely related to the kīkoʻo, the iconic board of traditional Hawaiian surfing. Originally made from native woods (and eventually redwood from the American Northwest), these large and heavy boards (typically eighty to a hundred pounds) were ideal for surfing the outer breaks of Waikīkī. It's easy to see why surfers like Duke were in such excellent shape. These athletes needed considerable strength just to carry these boards up and down the beach,

UMA
ʻŌWILI
PAHA
OMO
ʻŌNINI
ALAIʻA

KĪKOʻO
KĪOE
PUUA
DUKE MODEL
(KĪKOʻO)
WAIKĪKĪ
MODEL
(KĪKOʻO)

4

6

8

10

Above: Pōhaku riding a kīko'o at Ukumehame surf break, Maui

Opposite, top left: Youths with omo in Waikīkī, circa 1900

Opposite, top right: A modernized version of the alai'a by boardmaker Tom Wegener, based on traditional knowledge. It has an hourglass curve and wings at the tail.

Opposite, bottom right: Pōhaku paddling a 20-foot by 19-inch by 7-inch olo

Opposite, bottom left: Hawaiian man with a pu'ua, late 1800s

Following: Men with 'ōnini. Possibly Hilo, Hawai'i, or Waikīkī, O'ahu, circa 1890s.

in addition to paddling them out into the surf. Woe be the surfer who lost their board in a wipeout—they faced a potentially long swim back in. Once modern shapers introduced foam boards, kīko'o faded in popularity, but echoes of their size and shape are still found in the dimensions of modern surfboards.

⑩ **Olo.** Olo were twelve to twenty feet in length and weighed at least 150 to 200 pounds or more. The type of wood used made them sacred. Boards of this size were resource-intensive and therefore limited in number. For all these reasons, they were reserved for ali'i. The olo came in two distinct styles. One was completely elliptical, lengthwise and widthwise, so the nose was indistinguishable from the tail. The second style had similar contours, but with a pointed nose like the kīko'o. Board makers carved the olo from light woods like wiliwili or 'ulu (breadfruit) to help with buoyancy and reduce the overall weight. They immersed the board in the mud of an irrigated taro patch to waterproof the wood and add a pleasing dark stain.

The olo is made to ride giant swells that never break. Riding it is unlike riding any other board. Because it is so long and thick, it effectively has no top or bottom or front or back. If you try to turn the board, it will just laugh at you and keep going in whatever direction it's headed. The surfer is the one who must turn their body. It is also a struggle to paddle, and the surfer must sit much farther outside the break than usual. However, its almond-like convex shape means that it acts like the monohull of a boat. It planes through the water and gets up to speed much faster.

SIX TRADITIONAL STYLES OF HE'E NALU

Over the centuries, Hawaiians experimented with every size of board, style of wave, and riding position possible. However, they recognized six basic categories of wave-riding.

1. KAHA NALU: BODYSURFING

The first surfing. The foundation of it all. No board required.

Before anyone used a board to catch a wave, they used their body. In the Pacific Islands, bodysurfing was an integral part of ocean life. A visitor to Tahiti in 1866 wrote: "I have often seen along the border of the reef . . . 50 to 100 persons, of all ages, sporting like so many porpoises in the surf . . . cheering and animating each other; and by the noise and shouting they made, rendering the roar of the sea and the dashing of the surf comparatively imperceptible."

Kaha nalu is the most equal-opportunity form of wave riding. People who can't pop up on a board can still slide down a wave with their bodies. Even the gods bodysurfed. Despite this, bodysurfing never gained the same popularity in Western surf culture. For decades, it was a required skill for surfers who needed to retrieve runaway boards, but the invention of the surf leash in 1971 allowed them to skip it altogether.

However, true devotees speak passionately about kaha nalu's spiritual dimension. Mark Cunningham, world bodysurfing champion and North Shore lifeguard legend (he manned the Pipeline tower for twenty years!), said: "When you're

that low to the water, your sense of speed is just phenomenal. And it's not just riding the waves, it's swimming through them, it's diving under them. . . . Just the whole dance out there. You're like a piece of the ocean. I mean, what is the human body made of? Water. The physical makeup of the bodily fluids and the ocean is very similar. And now you've found each other. Hop on now, man, or you'll miss the train."

Previous: Nathan Florence at Pūpūkea, O'ahu

Above: Duke Kahanamoku body surfing at Waikīkī, 1930s

2. PAE PO'O OR PAIPO: BODYBOARDING

After bodysurfing, bodyboarding was the next logical step in the evolution of surfing. While lying prone is less practiced today, it was *the* most popular traditional style. Polynesians rode this way for centuries before they ever stood up. There were several very practical reasons.

Traditional boards had no fins, so lying prone allowed the rider to dip their hands and feet in the water to control direction and speed. Smaller boards are more maneuverable and can be used closer to shore, allowing more people to participate. While it may seem obvious, the biggest selling point of smaller boards is simply their size. Larger boards like the olo and alai'a were so heavy that no child could lift them. When they graduated to larger boards and standing up, that didn't mean surfers abandoned the style of their youth.

Smaller boards helped contribute to the spread of surfing as well. Early tourists who wanted to re-create the surf experience back in America couldn't exactly fit an olo board in their luggage, but they could transport the paipo boards used by children in Waikīkī. Decades later in 1971, shaper Tom Morey wanted to create a light, affordable imitation of the bodyboards that were popular in Kona, where hollow waves break close to rocky shores. Using a little foam and an iron, he created the boogie board, which has become the entry point to surfing for people of all ages all over the world.

Right: "I saw at this place for the first time, that famous sport of the natives, 'surf bathing.' . . . He dexterously flings himself into [a wave] . . . and with the speed of the wind rushes toward the shore, enveloped in a fleecy foam and spray. . . . It is the most exciting sport I ever witnessed." —John Wesley Bookwalter, Waikīkī, 1874

Following: Pypyr Luellen, somewhere in Kaua'i

3. HE'E NALU: STAND-UP SURFING

When most people think of surfing, this is what they imagine. However, Hawaiians didn't believe it to be better or worse than other styles. The earliest images of surfing depict large groups of people using every possible position.

Some of the disparity between Hawai'i's traditional surfing culture and modern surfing stems from early tourism art. The earliest popular images of surfing in the Western world came from Hawaiian tourism posters. Waikīkī was filled with Hawaiians bodysurfing and paipo-boarding. However, travel posters featured the more visually striking stand-up surfing, with the Waikīkī beach boys' muscular bodies on full display.

Those static images were misleading for other reasons as well. Standing the entire ride is typical nowadays, but it was not Hawaiians' preferred method. An early missionary noted, "Those who are expert frequently change their position on the board." Hawaiians switched between five basic positions: standing (kū), sitting (noho), kneeling (kukuli), lying down (kīpapa), and drop-knee (ho'okahi kuli). Modern Hawaiian surf contests devoted to upholding traditional culture emphasize this more mobile style. (See Buffalo's Big Board Surfing Classic, page 237.)

1830. The first Western image of people in the act of surfing.
Fittingly, on the left, is the first depiction of a wipeout.

4. HE'E ONE: SAND-SLIDING (SKIMBOARDING)

He'e one—riding the backwash of a wave over sand—has always been a popular activity for children. Their smaller frames make it easier to plane over the water's surface. However, skimboarding was popular for Hawaiians of any age. The lack of fins on traditional boards made it possible to slide with almost any size board.

Boards weren't even a requirement. Some children used banana leaves, and amazingly, adults could simply plank their bodies and body-skim down the sand. When Western goods arrived on the island, some creative souls began using hotel pillowcases and mattress covers. Stolen road signs worked, too.

Skimboarding has expanded its horizons and moved away from the ocean. Piggybacking on skateboard culture, skimmers have begun "urban skimming," using fountains, pools, and outdoor water spaces in cities.

Previous: On the left, Ulualoha Napeahi rides an alai'a. On the right is Ha'a Aikau. Rocky Point, North Shore, O'ahu.

Right: Waimea Bay, O'ahu, 1960s

Following: Outrigger Canoe Club beach boy Kalei sand skimming with a surfboard

5. HE'E PU'E WAI: SURFING FRESHWATER (RIVER-MOUTH SURFING)

Once you surf long enough, any water that forms a wave begins to look inviting. Nothing proves this better than he'e pu'e wai. When rivers swell during the rainy season and conditions are right, the rushing water creates stationary waves that are surfable. River waves occur only a couple of times a year (if at all), but Hawaiians and their gods enjoyed it to the fullest.

There once were several river waves across the islands. People river surfed in Hilo, Hawai'i, and Hāna, Maui, but the history of he'e pu'e wai reflects the history of Hawai'i. To increase agriculture, white landowners built irrigation canals to siphon off water from these rivers. Those waves were lost forever. The only surviving river wave is in Waimea, O'ahu.

Heavy winter surf pushes enough sand onto the beach to block the Waimea River's egress to the ocean. When the blocked river swells, the North Shore community bands together to dig a channel in the beach. When the river breaches, the force of the river combined with the elevation drop creates a wave that can be up to twenty feet tall. Some of the North Shore's best surfers (that is to say, some of the best in the world) ride this wave, but lifeguards warn amateurs away. The river can hurl tree branches and storm debris at the surfers, and its undertow is so strong that it can hold you underwater and rip you forty yards out into the bay. When you surface, you're right in the middle of the impact zone for the incoming waves. That's not where you want to be.

The river wave is one of Hawai'i's most unique cultural exports. In 1972, the city of Munich, Germany, engineered a stationary wave on its river, which proved so popular with surfers that the idea has spread to dozens of cities around the world. Now, thanks to he'e pu'e wai, surfing is no longer confined to the ocean but can be found right downtown.

WHEN THE RIVER BREAKS OPEN, ALL HELL BREAKS LOOSE.

—TERRY AHUE, NORTH SHORE LIFEGUARD

Waimea river break, O'ahu, 2025. On the left is Jamie O'Brien, one of the very few surfers to earn the unofficial title of "Mr. Pipeline."

6. PĀKĀKĀ NALU: OUTRIGGER CANOE SURFING

Opposite, top: Koa tree forest in Volcano National Park

Opposite, bottom: Hālau wa'a (canoe house) at Pu'uhonua o Hōnaunau

The canoe is the seed from which all Polynesian culture grows. It is the technology that gave Polynesians access to the ocean world, allowing them to expand beyond the limited space that island land provides. With a canoe, they could exist at sea—fishing, ferrying goods, fighting, recreating, and exploring. When voyagers reached the Hawaiian Islands, canoe building made another leap forward. Those first travelers encountered flora and fauna that didn't exist in their homelands. Previously unknown trees (like the koa) and birds (like the flycatcher and the crow) played a critical role in the evolution of the outrigger canoe.

The koa is endemic to Hawai'i and has unique properties. It is a hardwood that grows fast (five feet per year in its early stage) and wide (one inch a year). Other trees take generations to be canoe-worthy, but a koa is ready in as little as forty years. Earlier Polynesian canoes were typically made from planks lashed together, but Hawaiians could carve an entire hull from the koa's trunk, which made their canoes far stronger and more durable in heavy surf.

The construction of canoes was so important, time-consuming, and dangerous that it shaped Hawaiian language and culture. Mary Kawena Pukui and Samuel H. Elbert's *Hawaiian Dictionary* has 545 canoe-related entries. The people of Molokai believed that the mana of canoe builders was second only to that of ali'i. The building process was ritualized with prayers and offerings (pigs, red fish, even humans if the canoe was for an ali'i). Canoe builders had the help of at least fifteen different gods, including Kūpā'aike'e (Kū who eats the wood's crookedness; an adze god) and Kalālākamāhele (the far-reaching branch; she warned which direction a tree would fall so you wouldn't be crushed).

There were seven main steps to making a canoe: intention, tree selection, hewing the tree, carving the log, hauling the partially carved canoe, finishing the canoe, and dedicating the canoe. Fortunately, canoe builders had help from the birds as well. To avoid cutting down a tree only to find it was rotten, the kahuna kālai wa'a (master canoe builder) watched the birds. On Kaua'i, O'ahu, and Hawai'i, if an 'elepaio (flycatcher) pecked on a tree, it meant the tree was riddled with insects. On Maui and Molokai, the 'alalā (crow) performed the same function.

Koa was a plentiful and quickly renewable resource, so Hawaiians had plenty of raw material to work with, in a constant process of construction, experimentation, and invention. Hawaiians had over fifteen types of canoes, which they classified based on several factors—the number of hulls (single, double, or triple) and seats, and a canoe's size, length, shape, purpose, or hull material. Some canoes were designed for speed (kialoa, kiapā), fishing (kiapoko), or carrying baggage (pou). Others have unique features like specific outrigger floats (kaukahi) or weatherboards (leuwī). Sizes varied from twelve-foot canoes that carried two

Recognizing that the sea could be at once a friend and a killer, the ancient Hawaiian evolved a canoe form that may well be the most versatile and seaworthy rough watercraft ever designed or built by any culture at any time—a reflection of man in supreme harmony with his environment.

—TOMMY HOLMES, WATERMAN AND COFOUNDER OF THE POLYNESIAN VOYAGING SOCIETY

to six people to seventy-five-foot double-hulled canoes connected by a platform and paddled by twenty men.

And all the while, every day, every trip they made, they passed through the po'ina nalu (surf zone). If bodysurfing is the most elemental form of surfing, then pākākā is the most complex. It requires a team working in tandem to place a canoe that weighs hundreds of pounds on the exact tipping point where it will slide down the face of the wave. The results are spectacular.

Pākākā played a crucial role in introducing surfing to the world. When tourists began arriving in Waikīkī in the late nineteenth century, they were thrilled by the sight of Hawaiians surfing. They wanted to experience it for themselves but didn't have the water knowledge or the ability to use a surfboard. Canoe surfing was the perfect solution. For a small fee, they could ride along with Hawaiians (see Waikīkī Beach Boys, page 197). Their excited reactions in newspapers and postcards spread the word about the giddy rush of he'e, the slide. In some cases, this excitement caused them to abandon common sense. Local newspapers printed tales from bemused beach boys about tourists who wanted their money's worth. One man insisted that a guide take him and his wife out during a tropical storm. It didn't end well, and despite his protests, the man didn't get his money back. Canoe surfing in Waikīkī, in particular, has been so popular from ancient times to today that the surf break known as Kapuni was nicknamed Canoes. It is still the single most popular canoe-surfing site in the world.

I COULD NOT HELP CONCLUDING THAT THIS MAN FELT THE MOST SUPREME PLEASURE WHILE HIS [CANOE] WAS DRIVEN SO FAST AND SMOOTHLY BY THE SEA.

—WILLIAM ANDERSON, SURGEON, DESCRIBING CANOE SURFING IN TAHITI (1777)

Opposite: Buffalo Big Board Classic, Mākaha, O'ahu, 2024

Below: The transportation of a god-image by canoe paddlers wearing makini (ceremonial gourd helmets), 1778

A CANOE of the SANDWICH ISLANDS, the ROWERS MASKED.

H - 170 Surf Riding, Waikiki

THE WISDOM OF CANOES

Paddling a canoe requires strength, coordination, discipline, and teamwork. Because canoeing was an essential part of Hawaiian culture, the Hawaiian people accumulated significant wisdom from their experiences on canoes. Paddlers were packed closely together for lengthy periods of inter-island travel, and they needed to get along. Hawaiians preserved this wisdom in these ʻōlelo noʻeau.

Komo mai kāu māpuna hoe. Dip your paddle in. *Join in the effort.*

He poʻe hoʻopiha waʻa. Canoe fillers. *Useless people, like canoe riders who do nothing to help*.

He waʻa nahā i koʻokā kō kāne. A smashed canoe that has been buffeted by your husband. *Overindulgence in sex leads to impotence*.

ʻAʻohe waʻa hoʻohoa o ka lā ʻino. No canoe is defiant on a stormy day. *It doesn't pay to venture into the face of danger.*

Pae mai la ka waʻa i ka ʻāina. The canoe has come ashore. *Your desire has been fulfilled. Your hunger is satisfied. You are sated.*

Previous: Tourists on a canoe-surfing ride in Waikīkī, 1930s. This image was sold as a postcard by Kodak Hawaiʻi and proved so popular that it was in print for two decades.

Left: Buffalo Big Board Classic at Mākaha, Oʻahu, 2025

THE LANGUAGE OF SURFING

Surfing today is the same as it was a thousand years ago. You must paddle through the rolling surf, wait and watch for a wave, catch it, and slide. There are a LOT of wipeouts along the way. Surfers across the planet know surf words like *paddle-out, getting barreled,* and *wipe-out*. But Hawaiian is the original surfing language:

HOA HEʻE NALU

a surfing buddy

Oma or **hoʻōmo:** The paddle-out; to stroke or paddle with your hands.

Kīhē: The duck dive; diving under an oncoming wave to evade its surge.

Waho: Outside; beyond where the waves break, where you can sit on your board safely.

Kūlana: The lineup. No matter where in the world you surf, unless you are alone, you will paddle out to a lineup where surfers group and wait for a good wave to appear.

Kūlana nalu kū pono: The children's lineup. Surfing is a family activity in Hawaiʻi, so very small waves are reserved for keiki (children) and for inexperienced adults.

Nalu nui!: *Big wave!* Shouted when a good wave is spotted.

Hoʻoiho: The drop. Sliding down a wave from the peak to the bottom.

Hoʻi: Cutback. Turning back on the wave so you can stay in its most powerful area.

Lala and **muku:** To slide diagonally across the face of the wave and to return to the wave's curl, respectively. Lala and muku are fundamental moves, and descriptions of surfing often use them together:

Kahului Harbor, Maui

"Holo i ka **lala**, a **hoʻi** i ka **muku**" (Ride in a slide and cutback to return to the curl).

Uhi: Getting barreled. Literally, "to be covered or concealed by a wave."

Kā ʻia and **lumilumi ʻia:** Wipe out! Literally, "to be thrashed" and "to be pounded or crushed."

Kākelekele nalu: The glide; when you ride a wave for a long time without maneuvering, just enjoying the sensation.

Pae and **pae i ka nalu:** To catch a wave and to ride a wave into the shore, respectively. This is a highly praised skill, especially if you can step off onto the beach dry.

ʻŌ: To nose-dive your board; to pearl. For Hawaiians, the sound of someone nose-diving (which naturally leads to landing face first into the water) is quite literally: "Oooooo!"

Aea: To emerge from underwater. To break the surface so you can breathe again. A feeling of relief every surfer knows all too well.

E HOʻI KA UʻI O MĀNOA, UA AHIAHI:

Let the youth of Mānoa go home, for it is evening.

—ʻŌLELO NOʻEAU

Refers to the youth of Mānoa, who used to ride the surf at Kalehuawehe in Waikīkī. The surfboards were shared among several people who took turns using them. Those who finished first often suggested going home early, even though it might not be evening, to avoid carrying the boards to the hālau where they were stored. Later the expression became a description of anyone who went off to avoid work.

KŪLANA AND KULEANA

Kuleana is a cornerstone of Hawaiian culture—the set of rights and responsibilities or obligations that you inherit as a Hawaiian. Kuleana determines your role in your family, your community, and society. Traditionally, kuleana is primarily determined by four things: your birth order in your family (whether you are the youngest or the oldest, and whether your parent is a youngest or oldest child); family lineage (ruling or nonruling class); your relationship to place (locality and island where you were born and raised); and your family's occupation (fisher, farmer, canoe builder, healer, hula dancer, warrior, etc.).

When it comes to surfing, a relationship to a surf break is often generational. Some surfers have been surfing a break for their entire lives. They learned about that break from a member of the previous generation who was born and raised in that place. Respect for your elders is not limited to your family but extends to elders in the community.

The concept of belonging to a place is so important to Hawaiians that they have several words for it: *kama'āina* (land child, native-born), *keiki hānau o ka 'āina* (child born of the land, as in shaped by the land), *noho papa* (to live in a place for generations), *'ōiwi* (native to where your ancestors' bones rest), *kulāiwi* (native, native homeland), *one hānau* (birth sands). These terms apply only to those born and raised in an area (or who came as children), and who are familiar with its every aspect, including stories about its features, people, and gods.

From this cultural perspective, the existence and pecking order of a kūlana (lineup) makes much more sense. Generational surfers have precedence. If you are a newcomer to a surf break, you are expected to show respect—and most times, you will receive respect in turn. So what does that mean? Keep showing up, be humble, and ideally, the old-timers will notice your patience and reward you for it.

Kuleana plays a direct role in localism. *Localism* is a bad word in the surfing world. It refers to the aggressive behavior of locals toward malihini (newcomers) in a lineup. Localism occurs at surf breaks all over the world and can be a consequence of disrespect. If it's not your surf break, then you are a malihini to that break and should act according to kuleana. Give respect to receive respect.

WHEN YOU'RE A NEWCOMER TO A SURF BREAK, YOU SIT ON THE SHOULDER, WAIT YOUR TURN, AND BEFORE YOU KNOW IT, YOU'RE INVITED TO DINNER AND HAVING THE EXPERIENCE OF YOUR LIFE. YOU GET ALOHA WHEN YOU GIVE ALOHA.

—ANNE STONE, KAMA'ĀINA (LAND CHILD, NATIVE-BORN) OF KAILUA

PART 3

NALU LIFE

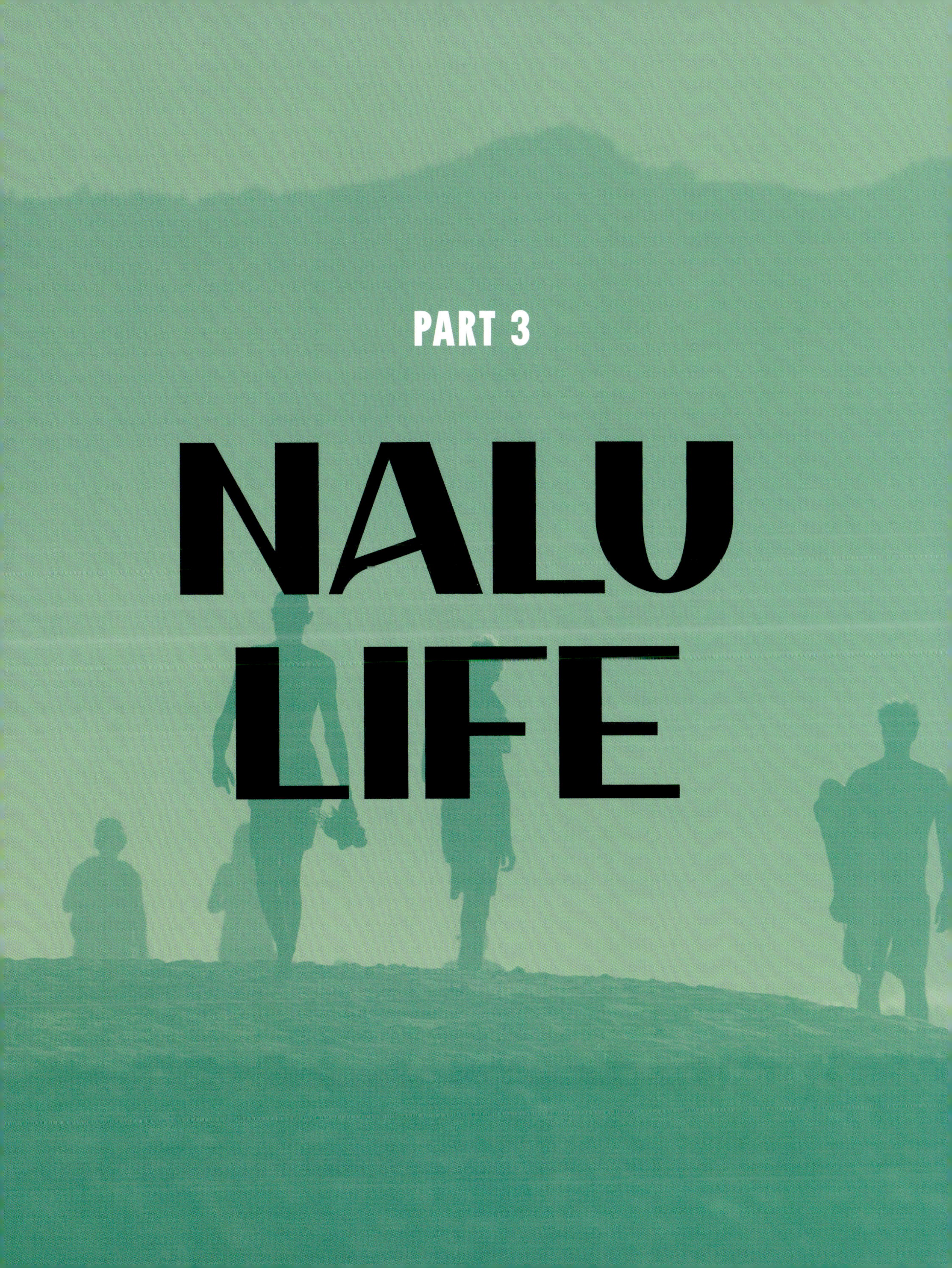

THE NATURAL WORLD AND AKUA

When early Polynesians explored the ocean and found new island homes, they didn't just bring plants and animals with them. They brought their gods and stories that gave shape and purpose to their world. Hawaiians inherited surfing from their Tahitian ancestors, who call it *fa'ahe'e*. Tahitians have a god of surfing, Huaouri, so it stands to reason that Tahitians continued to honor Huaouri when they settled Hawai'i, but there is no Hawaiian god of surfing. So what happened? Over time, the religion of these early Tahitian ancestors transformed until it became uniquely Hawaiian and certain gods were lost. Whether Hawaiians ever had a god of surfing remains a mystery, but they do have akua whose powers affect the surf. For example, coral reefs shape surf breaks and Hina-'ōpū-hala-ko'a (Hina-coral-passing-stomach), embodied in the coral polyp, is the mother of coral and spiny sea creatures. She appears as a woman and a coral reef. She is so important to the foundation of the island world that in the Kumulipo, an origin story, she is the first form of life—a coral polyp.

Opposite: Rosie Jaffurs, Chuns Reef, North Shore, O'ahu

Foremost among akua with ocean-related powers is Kanaloa. There are no waves without his ocean, currents, and winds. Kāne and Lono, who have storm-related powers, also affect the surf. Pele, who shapes the land with her lava and is a surfer herself, has several terrifying sisters who embody tsunamis. Nāmakaokaha'i is the most famous (see page 149). Then there are the Hi'iaka sisters. Hi'iaka-i-ka-'ale-kualono (Hi'iaka in the wave that overturns), Hi'iaka-i-ka-'ale-'uweke (Hi'iaka in the wave that uncovers), and Hi'iaka-wāwahi-lani (Hi'iaka heavenly destroyer) also cause tsunamis.

WHEN THE SURF OF ʻĀWILI WAS ROLLING DANGEROUSLY HIGH, ALL SURFING AND CANOEING CEASED, FOR THAT WAS A SIGN THAT THE GODS WERE RIDING.

—ʻŌLELO NOʻEAU

NĀMAKAOKAHA'I, THE GODDESS OF TSUNAMIS

Nāmakaokaha'i's tsunamis aren't just responsible for swamping the Hawaiian Islands from time to time, they're also responsible for Pele's migration to Hawai'i. After Pele seduced Nāmaka's husband, Nāmaka chased Pele with a tsunami all the way to Hawai'i. The battle between them continues to this day. Nāmaka's waves constantly pound Pele's island, and Pele retaliates by sending lava flows to the ocean.

'AUMĀKUA

Nature is both life-giving and death-dealing. The ocean is one of nature's most powerful forces. So not only did Hawaiians pray to akua for good surf, they also prayed for protection while out on the ocean. When it comes to ocean creatures, there are the good and the bad. Birds inspired early surfers to raise their arms to imitate flying. Sometimes dolphins will join surfers on a wave. Turtles are always fun to see.

As for sharks, you never know if they will ignore you or eat you (see "Shark Stories" on page 161). Fortunately for Hawaiians, they have 'aumākua (plural). An 'aumakua (singular) is an akua who is your relative. Much like guardian angels, they mainly guide and protect you. The first 'aumākua were gods who had children with humans. But a family could gain an 'aumakua by transfiguring a recently deceased relative into a nonhuman form—a ritual called kākū'ai. Sharks are the most common kind of 'aumākua because Hawaiians spend so much time in the ocean.

Above: White Sands Beach, Kailua-Kona, Hawai'i

Following: Harvest moon over Pipeline, O'ahu

ON THE NIGHTS WHEN THE TOPS OF WAVES SHINE WITH A GLISTENING LIGHT, IT IS SAID THE GODS HAVE JOINED IN THE SPORT.

—JUNE GUTMANIS

Ku'emanu Heiau, Kailua-Kona, Hawai'i Island

HEIAU

A heiau is a large stone structure or enclosure where gods are worshiped. There are different kinds of heiau: medicinal, agricultural, war and politics, and even surfing. Building them was incredibly labor intensive, requiring hundreds of people to line up and pass the stones along. Unfortunately, most of these heiau have either fallen into ruin or were dismantled and their stones repurposed.

On the slope of Lē'ahi (Diamond Head) overlooking Waikīkī sits Papa'ena'ena, a luakini (a heiau dedicated to war and politics). Papa'ena'ena already existed when Kamehameha conquered O'ahu in 1795. He sacrificed one of his rivals on it, and later his nephew (see page 177). But its location, with a view over the entirety of Waikīkī, also made it a perfect spot for a surf report. Hundreds of years before surfers could check an app on their phone to see when swell was on the way, the kahuna at Papa'ena'ena in the late eighteenth century raised a kite to signal ua pi'i ka nalu (Surf is up!). This chant describes the scene that followed:

Ke ʻOliʻoli o nā ʻLiʻi i Kalehuawehe

Hōʻae ka nalu nui o Kalehuawehe a hōʻae.
Ka ipu nui i lawe mai, ka ipu iki i waiho aku.
Hoʻolelelele lupe ke poʻo o Papaʻenaʻena
I hoʻokala ka nalu kūpono
ʻO ke kiaʻi mauka
Nānā ʻia ka ʻāhaʻilono,
A kūhea akua ka lono
ʻO ka mahi, ke kālai, ka hulumanu, āpau.
Lele ka hana, kiʻi nā papa
A neʻe i Waikīkī
Hoʻomū nā kānaka
I ka heʻe nalu
Lele papa, a kaha i ka ʻale
Kūhea aku i ka papa ʻenaʻena
E kūlaʻi i ka heʻe nalu
Mau ka manawaleʻa,
Alaila, paha mai ka Papaʻenaʻena
I ka nānā i ʻāpono ʻia.
Kūhea aku ka ipu nui, hoʻolei ka ipu iki
Hoʻi hou ʻo Kalehuawehe
Hoʻi hou ke kanaka i kuahiwi
ʻO ka heʻe nalu i Kalehuawehe lana mālie

The Delight of the Aliʻi at Kalehuawehe

Rise, the great surf of Kalehuawehe, rise.
The great gourd was brought forth,
the little gourd left behind
The head kahuna of Papaʻenaʻena flies the kite
To announce the excellent surf
The lookout in the uplands
Watches for the messenger
To call out the news
The farmers, the canoe carvers,
the bird catchers, everyone
Abandon work, grab boards
And go to Waikīkī
The people gather
To go surfing
Boards flying, cutting across the wave
Call to the raging surf,
To try and topple the surfer
The fun continues
Then the Papaʻenaʻena [kahuna] chants
About what is observed and confirmed,
Call to the large gourd, toss aside the small gourd
Kalehuawehe returns [to its former state]
The people return inland
The surf at Kalehuawehe floats serenely

As with all things related to surfing, location is a factor. You build a surfing heiau where there's good surfing, so there will be little time lost between praying for good waves and paddling out to meet them. Only two surfing heiau remain.

Haleʻaʻama Heiau is on the shore of Hōlualoa Bay, one of the best surf spots on Hawaiʻi Island. This heiau is part of a larger heiau compound named after Keolonāhihi, an aliʻi wahine who ruled Hawaiʻi Island around 1300 CE and who loved to surf. Most of the walls are in ruins, but they once provided an excellent view of the bay's amazing waves. This was a view that the local aunties took full advantage of for matchmaking (see Heʻenalu Hoʻohaʻihaʻi, page 189).

The Kuʻemanu Heiau, on the other hand, has been fully restored. It provides a perfect view of a popular surf spot in Kahaluʻu Bay in North Kona. Its location is ideally suited for surfers' needs, having once had a freshwater spring where they could rinse off when they emerged from the sea. Kahaluʻu waves were popular enough to inspire quite a few surfing rituals. There's a surfing stone called 'Ohū that surfers tapped while praying for good surfing conditions. There was a time, however, when the surf break's existence was under threat.

According to a legend, one day, the local menehune decided to turn Kahalu'u Bay into a giant fishpond. Menehune are little people, about two to three feet tall. They are very clever and incredibly strong, with a supernatural ability to quickly construct canoes and enormous stone structures.

Unfortunately, their plan to build a great wall in the bay would destroy the surf break. When the kahuna of Ku'emanu, Hinamoa, learned of their plans, he was determined to stop them and came up with a plan of his own. He knew the menehunes' one weakness. Despite their incredible talent for building, if they could not finish a project in a single night, they never returned to complete it. That night, Hinamoa hid himself and waited for the menehune to start building the wall. Then he began to crow like a rooster. The menehune heard him and assumed dawn was about to break, so they stopped working and never returned to finish the job. The surf break was saved, but the menehune's unfinished wall still stands today at Kahalu'u Bay.

Kahalu'u Bay, Hawai'i. Note the top right where the unfinished menehune wall still stands today.

TALK STORY TOUR

A GODDESS TURNS A SURFER TO STONE

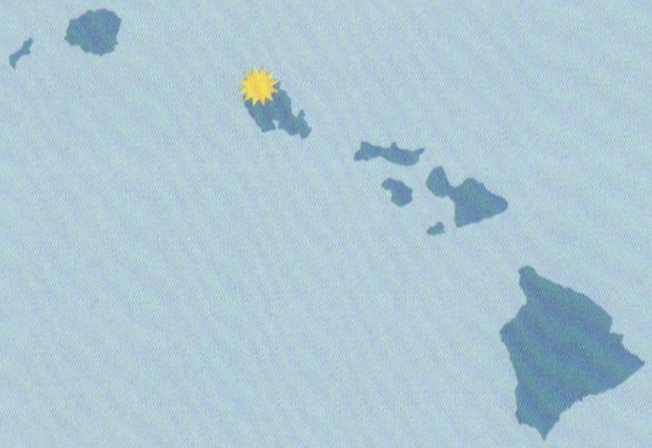

(NORTH SHORE, O'AHU)

Kahikilani, a warrior ali'i of Kaua'i, was an avid surfer. When he came to O'ahu, he brought his surfboard and his court, including his kahuna. As he surfed around O'ahu, he came across Paumalū. Hardly anyone surfed there because the waves were so dangerous, but after several attempts Kahikilani rode them with great success. Having conquered this break, he wanted a new challenge. Locals suggested he try Bird Island. If he managed to ride those waves, he would be the first to do so.

When Kahikilani arrived at Bird Island, birds began to circle and sing above him, praising his high rank and good looks. In a cave on a nearby cliff lived Ka'iulani, the foster daughter of a mo'o goddess. Ka'iulani had the power to understand birds. As she wove lehua lei, she heard them praising Kahikilani and went to look. She was instantly smitten. She asked the birds to carry a lei to him. Puzzled, Kahikilani asked his kahuna about the birds' strange behavior. The kahuna divined that a woman had used the birds to send him a lei. Kahikilani frowned. He had come to surf, not to find romance.

After conquering the surf of Bird Island, Kahikilani rested on the sand. Birds brought him more lei. Ka'iulani used her mana to give him the ability to understand birds, so when they sang about her beauty, he understood them. They praised Ka'iulani's enticing curves and silky hair that fell like a curtain about her body. They sang that her voice recalled gentle waves caressing the sand. Intrigued, Kahikilani followed them to her cave. Struck by Ka'iulani's beauty, he stayed.

Above: Gerry Lopez at Pipeline. Paumalū is the name of the surf break known today as Sunset and also the name for the land section that stretches along O'ahu's North Shore approximately from the surf breaks now known as Log Cabins up to Backyards, and includes such famous breaks as Pipeline, Sunset, Off the Wall, and Rocky Point.

He lived happily with her for some time, but soon his desire to surf the incredible waves at Paumalū made him restless. Before leaving, he promised to return and be true to her while he was away. But his surfing skills impressed another beautiful woman, and when she gave him a lei, he kissed her. The birds reported his betrayal. Livid, Ka'iulani rushed to Paumalū to confront him. She snatched the lei from his neck and replaced it with hers. Then she ended their affair and left.

Ashamed, Kahikilani tried to follow her to ask forgiveness, but she asked her mother to punish him. Her mother cast a spell that forced his legs to climb a steep ridge. Halfway up, he turned to look for Ka'iulani and transformed into stone. Kahikilani can still be seen today, staring after the woman he betrayed.

By the late 1800s, someone noted the stone's resemblance to George Washington's profile, so it also became known as the George Washington Stone.

TALK STORY TOUR

NEVER LAUGH AT AN AKUA WAHINE!

(WAILUA, KAUA'I)

On their first visit to the Hawaiian Islands from their homeland in Bora Bora, the goddess Kapō'ulakīna'u and her sisters toured Kaua'i in their wind forms. They flew over Wailua and saw people surfing where a river flowed into the ocean, so they decided to watch. Kapō called down a thick mist to hide them while they assumed human forms. People wondered about this unexpected fog and were astonished when it suddenly vanished, revealing several stunningly beautiful strangers dressed in red.

A group of handsome young men quickly stepped forward to invite them to surf and offered to lend them boards. The sisters accepted. As they all floated in the water waiting for a wave, Kapō told the men, "We should double up and surf together as couples on one board. When we're finished, we can go to your home and relax." The men quickly agreed. Just then, a large wave arrived. The couples gave such a thrilling display of skill that onlookers whistled and cheered.

When they landed ashore, several women placed lei on the heads and necks of Kapō and her sisters. The goddesses were delighted with their lei, but the men they had surfed with found their joy ridiculous and laughed at them. Irritated, Kapō suggested everyone should surf alone.

Once they were in the water, Kapō used her mana to call up a gigantic wave. As the wave rushed forward, it grew as high as a mountain. Terrified, people fled the beach. Kapō turned to the men and said, "Let each one show their skill. Go ahead—ride to shore!" Kapō and her sisters caught the wave successfully, but the men fell from its crest. The water dragged them down and battered them on the ocean floor.

Meanwhile, Kapō and her sisters glided ashore and waited for the ocean to spit the men out. When Kapō saw their bodies emerge in the white water near the river mouth, she turned them into stone. Then she and her sisters vanished. Only then did the people realize that these beautiful women were akua wāhine. You can still see these man-shaped stones when rough surf washes away the sand. They are known as the pae ki'i (row of images).

Opposite: Gerry Lopez, La Perouse, Maui

SHARK STORIES

When you live on an island, sharks are a natural part of life. They are always around, even when you don't see them. Sharks are such a powerful presence in the ocean that Hawaiians have deep respect for them. The ocean is the shark's home; you are just a visitor. Sharks attack, but if they are your 'aumakua, they also protect. All 'aumākua take offense when their human descendants harm the creatures they resemble. Offended 'aumākua either curse humans with an illness or kill them outright. Hawaiians who have a shark 'aumakua hold all sharks to be sacred, so they do not eat shark meat or harm sharks in any way. Hawaiians have many shark stories.

SHARK ATTACK, SURFER'S REVENGE

You may remember Kaulu, the demigod who tore apart giant waves with his bare hands to make waves small enough to ride (see page 41). He did that while searching for his brother, Ka'eha, who was kidnapped and enslaved by spirits. After Kaulu rescued Ka'eha, the spirits were furious and wanted revenge, so they challenged the brothers to a surf contest.

As the brothers paddled out to the surf break, the spirits commanded a shiver of sharks to feed Ka'eha to the great shark god Kū-kama-ulu-nui-ākea. Kaulu was too powerful to challenge directly, so the clever sharks waited for him to catch a wave. Once he was gone, they crowded around Ka'eha's board and drove him out to sea toward Kūkama. Ka'eha shook in terror. The shark's body was so long that Ka'eha couldn't see where it ended. When the shark opened his mouth, the bottom jaw rested on the ocean floor and the upper jaw reached the clouds, and his teeth were the size of coconut trees. Then Kūkama swallowed Ka'eha whole.

Meanwhile, Kaulu finished riding his wave and realized his brother was gone.

The spirits feigned ignorance, but Kaulu rightly feared a shark attack. He didn't have time to search the entire ocean, so he drank it dry, leaving nothing

Pavilions, Ho'okipa, Maui

HE MANŌ HOLO ʻĀINA KE ALIʻI.

The chief is a shark that travels on land.

The chief, like a shark, is not to be tampered with.

—ʻŌLELO NOʻEAU

TORPEDO
TORPEDO
WRS

SAVED BY A SHARK

In 1840, a severe storm sank a schooner in the perilous 'Alenuihāhā Channel. One passenger, Kaluahinenui, prayed to her shark 'aumakua to save her. When it appeared, she climbed on the shark's back and it carried her to the nearest island, Kaho'olawe.

but sea creatures flopping on the sand. Kaulu still did not see his brother, so he vomited the ocean back up.

Kaulu needed help from a greater power, so he flew up to the sky to where the star god Makali'i lived. He asked him what happened to his brother, and Makali'i ratted out the spirits. He pointed out a coral reef growing on the back of a shark large enough to be an island.

Kaulu flew down to the shark god and confronted him. "Have you seen Ka'eha?"

Kūkama said, "I have swallowed a man by that name. My stomach is digesting him."

Thinking quickly, Kaulu said, "Your mouth isn't big enough to swallow a man. You're just bragging."

Offended, Kūkama opened his mouth to show how mighty he was. Kaulu grabbed his jaws and held them open as he called into the shark for his brother. Ka'eha crawled out of Kūkama's mouth, but the stomach juices had already partially digested him. His skin was deeply wrinkled and not a single hair remained on his body.

Once Ka'eha swam to safety, Kaulu unleashed his fury. He dove into Kūkama's mouth, dug his fingers into the shark's body, and ripped out his heart. Kūkama writhed in agony as he sank to the ocean's floor. Kaulu calmly swam out of the hole he had torn in the shark's body and reunited with his brother.

When Kāne and Kanaloa learned of Kūkama's death, they were saddened because he was like a pet to them. They changed his spirit into stars and placed it in the sky. When Kūkama swims across the sky, he changes direction at midnight, so Hawaiians call him I'a-lele-i-aka (fish that jumps in the shadow). Elsewhere, this star cluster is known as the Milky Way.

KUIKUIPAHU, THE HAWAIIAN JONAH

Kuikuipahu was a famous ali'i of Kohala, Hawai'i Island. One day while he was surfing, a shark took him. Later, people found the shark beached at Kau'iki Hill, Hāna, Maui. To their shock, when they cut open the shark's stomach, they found Kuikuipahu still alive inside.

A KING'S RETRIBUTION

A few months after Captain Cook's death in 1779, a famine struck Kona. The king of Hawai'i Island, Kalani'ōpu'u, moved his court—family, attendants, warriors, advisors—to Kohala, where there was more food. The king, now in his eighties, desired nothing more than to amuse himself. His desire for endless feasts and hula began to drain the resources of the villages that hosted his court. His excesses displeased two powerful ali'i, who began to plot his removal.

Rumors of this possible uprising reached Kalani'ōpu'u, but he feared only one man—Nu'uanupā'ahu, an ali'i of Ka'ū, who had accompanied him to Kohala. The king conferred with his kahuna, who came up with a plan. Nu'uanapā'ahu had to die, but his death had to seem like an accident. So they prayed for their gods to send a shark to kill him.

A few days later, huge sets rolled in at Kapaelauhala in Kohala. Nu'uanupā'ahu paddled out on his alai'a board and caught a wave. He rode the wave all the way to shore; then he went back out and caught a second one. But this time a shark rode it with him, its mouth wide open, water streaming through its sharp teeth and gills, as it flew at him like a mālolo fish. Witnesses reckoned the shark to be thirty-six feet long, and they fled the water in terror.

When Nu'uanupā'ahu saw the shark, he slid his board up to the crest of the huge wave, but the shark pursued him. Pushing himself to the limits of his skill, he shot across the wave like an arrow in flight and passed over the shark. As he flew over the shark, it jerked around to bite him, but he punched its eye, and the shark dropped back down in the water.

Nu'uanupā'ahu cut back across the hollow of the towering wave and passed over the shark. Once again, the shark attacked, but Nu'uanupā'ahu shot past it. When the shark twisted to bite him, he shoved his hand into its gills and tore them out. The wounded shark abandoned the fight, and Nu'uanupā'ahu caught a wave back to shore.

Before Nu'uanupā'ahu could reach safety, another shark attacked him. He tried to fight it off by pounding it with his fists, but the shark tore off one of his buttocks. Despite his horrible injury, he made it to shore. Witnesses were amazed that he was still alive and shouted praise for his courage and strength. When Nu'uanupā'ahu's kahuna reached him, they found shark gills in his hand and immediately began to pray the sharks to death: "On this day, these sharks will die and wash ashore, where pigs and dogs will eat them as they rot and stink." The mana of their words was so great that they withered the leaves of the surrounding trees. That same day, one shark washed ashore at Nā'ohaku and the other shark at Hāpu'u. As for Nu'uanupā'ahu, he succumbed to his injuries. With his death, the rebellion ended.

THE LITTLE GUARDIAN

In 1848, as Kehopu was paddling his canoe to join his friends who were fishing for 'ōpelu (mackerel) offshore of Pa'akō in Maui, he heard an alarming smacking noise behind him. To his horror, when he turned around, he saw the gaping mouth of a shark—twice the length of his canoe—about to swallow him. Just then a little shark appeared and placed itself between Kehopu's canoe and the big shark. Undeterred, the bigger shark swam to the other side of the canoe, flipped it over with its head, and began biting the outrigger. Kehopu climbed onto the canoe hull but struggled to keep his grip as the big shark continued its savage attacks. The other fishermen were too frightened to help. Certain he was about to die, Kehopu prayed to the gods to ask forgiveness for any offenses he might have committed.

After the big shark tore off the outrigger, it went to bite Kehopu, but the little shark shoved the big shark's mouth away. Every time the big shark attacked, the little shark blocked it—until the big shark finally lost interest and swam away. Once it was gone, the nearest fishermen paddled over to pull Kehopu into their canoe. All the fishermen agreed that the determined little shark was surely Kehopu's 'aumakua.

TALK STORY TOUR

KE KAI O MĀMALA

THE SEA OF MĀMALA

(HONOLULU, O'AHU)

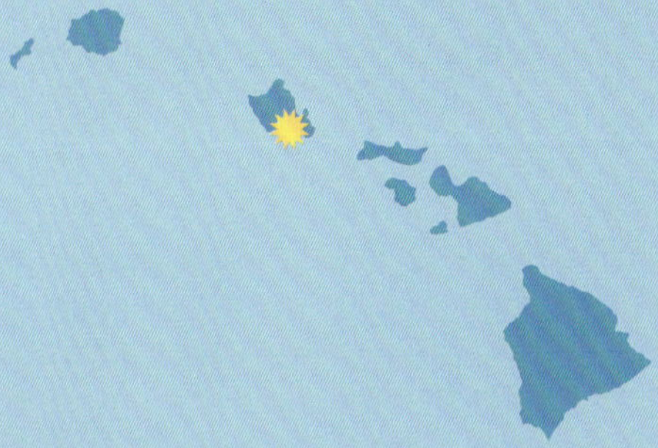

Māmala was a shark shapeshifter, famed for her beauty and skill at surfing. Because she enjoyed the company of humans, she kept her true nature a secret. Māmala surfed the stretch of ocean from Kou (known today as Honolulu Bay) to just before Waikīkī. Her favorite break was far offshore of Kou, where strong winds whipped the sea into a frenzy. She took great delight in surfing the rough, whitecapped waves that rolled toward the shore in disorderly sets.

Māmala was famous for wearing a lei on her head when she surfed. People gathered to admire her incredible feats of surfing and placed bets on whether she'd lose her lei, but she never did.

When Māmala wasn't surfing, she relaxed in the shade of a coconut-tree grove on the sands of Kuloloia. There she played kōnane (Hawaiian checkers) with her sweetheart, a surfer named 'Ouha, who was also a shark shapeshifter. One day, much to 'Ouha's dismay, Māmala left him for Honoka'upu, a handsome ali'i of Kou. Brokenhearted, he spent the rest of his life as a shark, patrolling the waters from Hanauma Bay to Lē'ahi.

Māmala continued to surf that spot, so people called the waters from Kou to Waikīkī the Sea of Māmala. Her sea still exists, but in the 1930s, the government built a harbor that destroyed many of the surf breaks she enjoyed.

Opposite: Alicia Kelley at Ala Moana Bowls, O'ahu

ALI'I

Ali'i were some of the most enthusiastic, well-resourced, and gifted surfers in history. While pretty much all Hawaiians surfed, ali'i had the most valuable commodity of all—free time. The one ironclad rule of surfing is that the only way to improve is to spend time in the water. They had servants who freed them from the everyday duties of farming, fishing, hunting, and cooking. Plus, in a culture that viewed surfing as a way of displaying mana, earning praise, showing courage, and defeating opponents, it was important for an ali'i to be good at it. Forget the expensive luxury surfing package tours that exist today. With ample free time, total authority, and the pick of some of the best waves on the planet, the ali'i crafted the ultimate surfing experience for themselves. They had an entire style of board all to themselves that enabled them to catch not only the biggest waves, but also the ones farthest out from shore (see olo, page 107).

In 1810, Kamehameha I became Kamehameha the Great. Through a combination of warfare, political maneuvering, and fulfilled prophecies, he became the first ruler to unify the Hawaiian Islands into one kingdom. Two years later, Kamehameha moved the center of his kingdom from O'ahu to Kamakahonu Bay in Kailua-Kona, where he spent the last years of his life. This area was also home to his favorite surf break: Ko'okā (to be tossed violently).

Being royalty had many advantages. Ali'i did not have to walk and carry their boards to a surf break or even paddle out if they didn't want to. Kamehameha, usually accompanied by his favorite wife, Ka'ahumanu, would order his canoe paddlers to row them out to Ko'okā. This was not a leisurely outing. John Papa 'Ī'ī, who served in Kamehameha's household, warned that surfing there was dangerous: "Any timid person . . . was overwhelmed and could not reach the landing place." Ko'okā is known to break only when waves are big, but Kamehameha was unusually skilled at picking the best waves to ride. Once he spotted a wave that met his approval, his paddlers, the most

Kauhola Point Lighthouse, Kohala Coast, Hawai'i. Just to the left of this photo is a bay which has the surf break known as Lighthouse (for obvious reasons). The wave pictured here is known as Swimming Pools and is rarely surfed. Photographer Bryan Lowry explains, "It's best at 8- to 10-foot Hawaiian [i.e., local way of gauging wave height; others would refer to these as 16- to 20-foot waves], but sketchy as hell. You always do a shark check before paddling out for dawn patrol. If a cow falls into the ocean from the cliffs, it's a feeding frenzy. I've seen it."

skilled on the island, maneuvered the canoe to catch the onrushing wave. The king and queen grabbed their boards and launched themselves off the canoe onto the already-breaking wave. This form of surfing is called lelewa'a (canoe-leaping), a favorite pastime of theirs.

The surfing world usually credits the invention of tow-in surfing to the big-wave surfers known as the Strapped Crew (Laird Hamilton, Dave Kalama, Darrick Doerner, and others) in the 1990s. But Hawaiians thought of it long ago.

When Kamehameha and Ka'ahumanu surfed, they had the waves all to themselves because those waves became kapu. When the ride was over, the king and queen paddled back out or their canoe paddlers ferried them back to the surf break so they could go again.

Whenever Kamehameha and Ka'ahumanu visited new surf breaks, they asked local surfers to advise them on how to best read and ride those waves. The surfing world usually credits the idea of using spotters on land to big-wave surfers like Garrett McNamara, the first to ride the monsters at Nazaré, Portugal, in 2010. But when Ka'ahumanu first surfed at Maliu in Kohala, the local surf expert, Kekakau, stood on the shore and waved a white flag to indicate where she should land for each wave. As he watched the sets coming in, he moved the flag to show her where the best waves were coming and how she could adjust.

When ali'i decided to surf, their servants would often fire up the imu (underground oven) to cook food, so that by the time the surf session was done, a meal awaited them. One surf break near Hilo is even known as Kaloaoka'oma (the length of the oven).

This all demonstrated one indisputable fact—it was good to be an ali'i.

KAI O KE ALI'I.

Sea of the chief.

A surf spot reserved for ali'i.

PERSONAL CHANTER

Many ali'i had chanters in their court to honor them. That included praising their surf skills—but not always. It was a tradition in some places, but not in others. Keawe, the ruler of Hawai'i Island, and his servant found this out the hard way. They had no such tradition at their home. When they traveled to Kaua'i, Keawe went out in the water with the local ali'i to surf. Meanwhile, Keawe's servant became nervous when he saw local servants chanting in praise of their ali'i whenever they rode a wave all the way to shore. The servant knew that if he didn't come up with a chant, Keawe would be shamed in front of the other ali'i. So the servant listened to what the locals were saying and hurriedly improvised a chant in their style, but he didn't quite know what to say, so he stuck to generic statements:

O ka hana a Keawe
A o ko Keawe hana,
A o ko Keawe inoa.

Keawe's surfing feat,
And Keawe's other feat,
And Keawe's name!

Basically, the chanter is saying: "Whoa, Keawe just pulled a sick move! / And another sick move! / Yeah, Keawe is his name—respect!"

TALK STORY TOUR

SURFING WAS HER GREATEST PLEASURE

(HAMAKUAPOKO, MAUI, AND ʻEWA, OʻAHU)

Keleanohoanaʻapiʻapi was known for two things: her great beauty and her incredible skill as a surfer. Born sometime in the sixteenth century, she was the daughter of an aliʻi kāne from Maui and an aliʻi wahine from Kauaʻi. Her greatest pleasure was surfing at Hamakuapoko on Maui. Word of her grace on wave caught the ear of Lo Lale, an aliʻi of Oʻahu. Lo Lale desired a wife, so he sent his attendants to kidnap Kelea. They paddled to Maui, grabbed her, and brought her back to Lo Lale's hometown in upland Oʻahu, far from the sea, where he made her his wife. For ten years, Kelea did not see the ocean, feel kai on her skin, or hear the roar of a breaking wave.

The tenth year, Kelea convinced Lo Lale to allow her to travel to see the ocean at ʻEwa. When she heard the roar of the surf and saw riders on the waves, joy flooded her heart. She borrowed a board, and as she paddled out into the water, her ten-year absence seemed to wash away. From her very first wave, people onshore saw the skill and beauty of her surfing and burst into cheers so loud that the noise rolled up the hills to the farmlands where the aliʻi Kalamakua was visiting. When he learned the reason for the celebrations was the graceful surfing of a beautiful stranger, he went to see for himself.

Kalamakua arrived on the beach just in time to see Kelea ride a wave all the way to shore and step onto the sand, her naked body glistening. Kalamakua was so awestruck that he removed his kīhei (a long cloak or shoulder cape) and wrapped it around her hips. Then and there, he asked her to marry him, and she agreed. She never returned to Lo Lale and spent the rest of her days by the sea.

Kelea's influence continues today. Her granddaughter was Kalāʻaiheana, the daughter of Piʻilani, supreme ruler of Maui. Upon Kalāʻaiheana's death, her family deified her into a moʻo named Kihawahine, who became their war deity. In 1795, Kamehameha elevated Kihawahine to an akua for the entire nation. Certain families today trace their lineage back to her.

Opposite: Ashley Nielson at Shark Pit, Lahaina, Maui

ME'E NO HE'E NALU: Surfing Hero

QUEEN KA'AHUMANU

(1768–1832)

When British sailors first witnessed surfing, they were fascinated. In 1795, the first lieutenant on the *Discovery*, Peter Puget, noted that one Maui ali'i wahine, Nāmāhana, was one of the best surfers in the islands. Clearly a talent for surfing ran in the family, because her daughter Ka'ahumanu became one of Hawai'i's most famous surfers.

Ka'ahumanu was born into a powerful family, a descendant of kings and queens from both parents. Her father, Ke'eaumoku, was Kamehameha's advisor, and Ka'ahumanu grew up in his court. As she matured, so did her beauty, and Kamehameha took her as his wife. When Captain George Vancouver met Ka'ahumanu in 1794, he described her as "one of the finest women we have yet seen on any of the islands."

Ka'ahumanu quickly became Kamehameha's favorite wife, which she remained for the rest of his life. He taught her everything he knew about surfing. She took to it with a passion and became his constant surfing companion.

Many of Ka'ahumanu's exploits have already been noted—her love of canoe-leaping, surfing all day, and using spotters to guide her. Ka'ahumanu was not unusual in that sense—all ali'i surfed—but we know about her exploits because missionaries introduced literacy during her lifetime, and a court attendant, John Papa 'Ī'ī, recorded them. What makes Ka'ahumanu's story exceptional is when her position, power, and love of surfing merged into one of the most dramatic moments in Hawaiian history.

Around 1812, Ka'ahumanu had an affair with her husband's handsome nephew, Kanihonui. Kamehameha was not pleased. He had Kanihonui executed and left to rot in the Papa'ena'ena Heiau on the slope of Lē'ahi. Ka'ahumanu was beside herself with grief and contemplated overthrowing her husband and giving the kingdom to his heir, Liholiho, who was barely in his teens.

Here's the backstory. Ka'ahumanu was politically astute from an early age and steadily gained political influence through her familial connections with many powerful ali'i. Before her father died, he warned Kamehameha that she was the only person who could wrest power from him. When Ka'ahumanu called her clan to Waikīkī to grieve Kanihonui's death, the king perceived this as a direct threat. 'Ī'ī wrote: "Before she laid her plans for the war, a holiday for the purpose of surfing at Kapua [now known as Old Man's and Kaimana Beach] in Waikīkī was proclaimed, because the surf was rolling fine then." Ka'ahumanu chose that spot because it gave her a full view of the heiau where her lover's body lay rotting. She and her clan passed the day "surfing, lamenting, and surfing" while drinking liquor.

Meanwhile, Kamehameha ordered his warriors to line the beach and stand guard in case surfing turned to war.

As evening fell, Ka'ahumanu came out of the water and heard her cousin ask Liholiho if he wished to overthrow his father. 'Ī'ī wrote, "When the boy heard this, he bowed his head and meditated on the nature of the question." After a moment, he looked up, and said, "I do not want my father to die." Everyone respected his answer, and the surfing memorial ended peacefully.

THE MOST EXPERT

"Nammahana [Nāmāhana], the wife of Toyomodu [Ke'eaumoku], who is reckoned one of the most expert at that Diversion [surfing] immediately Stript naked and she certainly notwithstanding her Corpulency performed her part with wonderful Dexterity. The first Sea or Surf that brought her in towards the Beach was immensely high, on its Top she came, floating on a Broad Board till the Break[er] had nearly reached the Rocks, she then suddenly turned, went under that & the one following and so on till she had regained her Situation at the back of the whole. Then she waited for a large Swell and once more performed her part with great Expertness."—Peter Puget, quoted in *The Voyage of George Vancouver: 1791–1795*

HEIHEI NALU

SURFING COMPETITIONS

The Hawaiians of old lived for sport competitions. It didn't matter if it was footraces, wrestling, boxing, hōlua sledding, ʻulu maika (Hawaiian bowling), spear throwing, surfing, or any other traditional sport. Betting on sports is a firmly established tradition in Hawaiʻi. They wagered canoes, fishing nets and lines, clothing, pigs, chickens. They even bet their lives. If they lost, the victor could either make them their lifelong servants or kill them outright.

Surfing competitions were by far the crowd favorite. Duke Kahanamoku recalled that "people would gather from near and far; especially if a famous surf rider from another district or island was seeking to wrest honors from their own champion." The rules were not set in stone. If the contest was between two people, the challenger set the rules. When it came to large competitions, the organizers set them.

Once all bets were laid, surfers paddled out and waited for a wave to catch together. When the right one came along, one of them might yell, "He ua!" (It is raining), their version of "Ready, go!" Then, they took off on the wave together.

Contestants were judged not only on their ability to ride the waves but also on their maneuvers on the board itself. Frequently changing positions was seen as a sign of an expert rider. Another challenge involved distance; competitors would compete to see who could ride the same wave the farthest and fastest. By the late 1800s, some events included buoys along the course to help spectators judge. Hawaiian history is rich with stories of surfing contests that aimed to prove one's worth, settle personal vendettas, or eliminate enemies.

Opposite: Kua Bay, Hawaiʻi Island

I WAI NOʻU.

Give me water.

—ʻŌLELO NOʻEAU

An expression used to challenge someone to a contest.

THE BODYSURFING CONTEST BETWEEN ʻUMI-A-LĪLOA AND PAʻIEA

Before 'Umialīloa became supreme ruler of Hawai'i Island sometime in the 1400s, he lived a humble life. While 'Umi was living in Hilo, he and his friend Koi went to Laupāhoehoe, where they saw people bodysurfing. Several spectators praised the skill of a minor ali'i named Pa'iea, but 'Umi was unimpressed. He whispered to one of the admirers, "Is that the best Pa'iea can do, just rise with the surf and fall back again? That is not the way we surf in our land. One must ride clear to the edge of the beach before we call him an expert." 'Umi's critique reached Pa'iea, who was not pleased. Who was this upstart not yet old enough to grow a proper beard? Pa'iea challenged him to a bodysurfing contest and bet him a life of servitude. Pa'iea fully expected that he would refuse such high stakes and 'Umi would thus be humiliated. But to his shock, 'Umi accepted.

Annoyed, Pa'iea changed the bet. He noticed 'Umi's whale-tooth pendant and bet two double canoes and a single canoe against it. Again, 'Umi accepted. So Pa'iea upped the bet once more to humiliate 'Umi. He wagered four double canoes instead of two. Just then, a wealthy young man of Laupāhoehoe offered to back 'Umi and the deal was set. The two men agreed to bodysurf the same wave to demonstrate their skills. As they rode the wave, Pa'iea slammed into 'Umi's shoulder to push him against a coral outcropping in the middle of their path. Seeing the danger, 'Umi shifted his body and passed it on the inside. This maneuver shot him to victory. When Koi saw the bruise on 'Umi's shoulder, he was furious and whispered a vow to 'Umi—one day he would kill Pa'iea for his insolence.

After 'Umi became king, he put his friend in charge of Puna and asked him to fulfill his vow. When Koi returned with Pa'iea's corpse, 'Umi offered it as a sacrifice at a heiau.

Previous: The Cave in Honolua Bay, 1976. This break got its name from a small cave in the nearby cliff that would eat surfboards in the days before leashes.

SAVED BY A CHANT

Nāihe was Kamehameha's advisor and chief orator. He was also such an expert surfer that some ali'i were jealous of his surfing skills and wanted to kill him. They invited him to a surfing competition for ali'i in Hilo. They established a rule that surfers could go ashore only if someone praised their surfing skills in a chant. They told everyone about the rule except for Nāihe. It was only once he was in the water that he learned about this rule, so he had no way of informing his chanter, an old woman who had served him his entire life.

That day, the surf was extremely rough. After hours of surfing, Nāihe was the last one in the ocean, and he was exhausted. An ali'i from Puna took pity on him and ordered his servant to tell Nāihe's attendant about the danger her master was in. The servant found the old woman asleep on the beach. When she heard what was happening, she began to sob. She hobbled to the water to save her beloved ali'i. She took one look at the rough surf and improvised a chant.

Hawaiians consider this surf chant the best example of this genre. The chanter's opening lines poetically refer to the waves as a majestic malo (loincloth) for Nāihe. The line "Rise and gird the loincloth" is said when preparing for an important endeavor. As Nāihe rode each wave, his loincloth flew behind him because he was going so fast. She also honors his surfboard, Halepo. She even inserts a subtle insult for those who plotted her master's demise: "the surf of Kuhihewa (error in judgment)."

The great waves, the great waves that rise from Kona,
The exalted loincloth,
The long swelling wave rolls steadily toward the shore until your loincloth flies,
The splendid loincloths follow one behind another.
The sea loincloth, loincloth of the ali'i.
Rise and gird the loincloth,
Strike the sea on the day of the board Halepo.
Halepo mounts the wave,
The wave from Kahiki rises,
An immense wave, a swelling wave,
Swelling up to break, the wave rises and then dashes
The surfing spray rises
Rough receding surf of the island,
The smiting surf of the great wave,
The foamy breakers of Hikiau.
A surf to ride when the sun is highest,
Strikes the coral, the coral head inland,
The surf of Kuhihewa strikes fiercely,
Strikes the coral, the shoreward coral head,
Strikes the reef, cracks it,
Violently cracking and wrenching it,
As it yields, it shakes tremendously,
The expert's skin is not slick.

Once her chant ended, Nāihe was able to come ashore, exhausted but alive because of an ali'i's compassion and a chanter's talent. Thus did Nāihe survive this attempt to kill him. He eventually died of natural causes in December 1831.

BATTLE OF THE SEXES

On June 11, 1877, Kamehameha Day celebrations at Lahaina included a surf competition. The *Hawaiian Gazette* reported:

> Poepoe, the champion surf rider of Hawaii, took part in this contest, and there was a murmur among the spectators as this splendid athlete appeared on the beach with his board that the judge of the games might as well give him the prize at once. But there was another, and very special matter of interest in this contest;—a woman was to contend with men in this daring and dangerous pastime. Though past her youth . . . this woman was of a comely form, which was but slightly concealed by the scant pa-u [sarong]. Her long flowing hair, and well rounded limbs glistened pleasingly through the green translucent white crested combers, through which she lightly made her way seaward, along with three stalwart male companions, till they reached the outer line of surf swell. This surf is grand at times in Lahaina; and the old gods wanted the old capital to have a treat this day. The towering, combing waves rushed and thundered like an avalanche upon the beach. Now those bold navigators on their tiny craft, are waiting for a great swell. Here it comes . . . the swelling long liquid ridge arises. It towers aloft and rushes onward to engulf the shore. And onward came the children of old ocean,—coming,—sliding, and dancing on her crests. Poepoe with outstretched arms like an ancient warrior about to hurl a spear, comes erect on his swift flying keel; but where is Nakooko, the woman?—Keeping her tiny craft well aslant the insurging tide, she shoots like a flying fish through the whitening foam, and. . . . jostles the champion on his wonted plank of victory, and so the flowing hair and the rounded form came in foremost amid out-cries of a delighted multitude glad that the woman had won.

Opposite: Vaihitimahana Inso at Ala Moana Bowls in Honolulu, O'ahu

HE'ENALU HO'OHA'IHA'I

SURFING TO FLIRT

Surfing is sexy. There's no denying it. There are men and women exhilarated by the elements and the adrenaline rush of catching a wave, wearing very little, bodies glistening with sea spray. Hawaiians even have a word for that slick-skinned look: *lalilali*. They also understood that people may go out into the ocean looking for a lot more than a wave. They called it he'enalu ho'oha'iha'i—surfing for the purpose of flirting.

Although Hawaiians frequently surfed naked, when they were trying to catch the eye of someone, they appreciated the power of standing out from the crowd. A surfer on the prowl would let everyone know by wearing red. The women wore red sarongs, which molded to their curves when wet. The men wore red loincloths, which was the look warriors adopted before going into battle. Not only did it invoke one of the most masculine images in the culture, but it also highlighted their . . . endowments.

It wasn't just the wet clothing that raised the temperature of the lineup. The movement of bodies on the undulating sea was not lost as a metaphor for lovemaking. A beautiful woman might liken her body to a surfboard ridden by her lover:

'O ka papa he'e nalu kēia,
pāhe'e i ka nalu ha'i o Makaiwa.

This is the surfboard that will slide
on the rolling surf of Makaiwa.

And men had a saying of their own:

'O 'oe ka papa, 'o wau ka he'enalu,
he'ehe'e mālie kāua.

You are the board, I am the surfer,
we gently slide.

Not only was everyone looking good out in the water, they all knew it, too. They were ready for action in whatever way the ocean or hormones moved them.

Unlike nowadays, when the rule of one person/one wave is the norm, Hawaiians frequently rode "party waves." But when young men wanted to catch someone's eye, they would shun the crowd and wait for a wave they could ride solo, the better to show off their smooth moves and buff bodies. When a man and a woman did finally catch each other's eye, they sealed the deal by riding the same wave. Once they stepped off that wave onto land, their next steps often led to someplace more secluded.

On Hawai'i Island, a goddess, Waka, tried to use this rule to her advantage. Her human granddaughter, Lā'ieikawai, was the most sought-after woman in the islands and was constantly fending off suitors who surfed to get her attention. Eventually, Waka found the perfect match, a handsome high-ranking ali'i, and was eager to make it happen. She told Lā'ieikawai to catch the same wave as the ali'i and even offered to set the mood: "After the surf riding, then I will send the birds and a mist over the land; this is the time for you to return with your husband to your house, to become one flesh according to your wish."

Little did Waka know that a local youth, Halaaniani, who was known for his good looks but selfish spirit, wanted Lā'ieikawai as well. His sister, a goddess, used her mana to confuse Lā'ieikawai into sharing the wave and then a bed with him, the wrong man (see "Marital Wipeout").

Waka wasn't the only grandmother to recognize the power of surf breaks for matchmaking. Hale'a'ama, the surfing heiau at Kona, was more than a place to pray for good waves. Its stone walls were a convenient perch for aunties to observe young folk mingling and strutting their stuff in the water. The aunties would discuss who would make a good couple and then use their mana to speak that romance (and future children) into existence. When that new generation paddled out into the surf, a new generation of aunties was there to help them find love, too.

MARITAL WIPEOUT

Using a goddess to steal a wave and a wife isn't the best start to a marriage, and for Halaaniani and Lā'ieikawai, it didn't get better. Lā'ieikawai had a twin sister, Lā'ielohelohe, and after four months of marriage, Halaaniani began to desire her, too. He needed time to seduce her, so he told his wife: "Ever since we have lived up here, my delight in surf riding never ceases. At noon, the longing seizes me; it is the same every day." He used his supposed surfing trips to seduce his wife's sister. Unsurprisingly, his wife eventually dumped him.

Duke Kahanamoku, Honolulu, Oʻahu, 1912

Surfing was a pastime that displayed men and women's expertise, but not only that. It also revealed who were attractive men and women, and looking over their every feature gratified the eyes—that was why the ali'i and the people enjoyed surfing.

—SAMUEL MĀNAIAKALANI KAMAKAU

TALK STORY TOUR

KALAMAINU'U, THE LIZARD GODDESS WHO SURFS TO FIND HUSBANDS

(COMING TO A LINEUP NEAR YOU)

Kalamainu'u is a notorious mo'o akua who still roams the islands today. As a human, she is breathtakingly beautiful. As a lizard, she is terrifying. She looks like a Komodo dragon, but bigger, and she surfs by riding her tongue, which transforms into an olo board.

She hides her true nature in the presence of humans, because her greatest pleasure besides surfing is handsome men. She prowls the islands on her surfboard looking for love.

Kalamainu'u has taken many husbands over the course of her long life (she is practically immortal). The men she chooses have no idea that this beautiful woman is a lizard goddess. Because she is afraid to lose them, she keeps them like prisoners—she caters to their every need but forbids them from leaving her sight. By that point, they *do* suspect that she is a goddess, so they obey her, but these men never last long. Kalamainu'u has a terrible temper, and when she loses it, she eats her husbands.

Only one man survived—Puna'aikoa'e. There are three versions of the story about Kalamainu'u and Puna'aikoa'e. Depending on the version, Kalamainu'u lives in a cave somewhere on Molokai, at Mokulē'ia (O'ahu), or at Waimānalo (O'ahu). Also depending on the version, she finds Puna'aikoa'e while surfing at Kukui (Waimānalo) or Kalehuawehe (Wailua, Kaua'i). In the Kukui version, she uses her powers of seduction to keep his attention on her as they paddle across the ocean from O'ahu to Molokai.

In all versions, Puna survives only because Kalamainu'u's brothers help him escape. They advise him to flee to Hawai'i Island and seek protection from Pele, one of the few who are powerful enough to oppose their sister's wrath. Pele was sure to help him because she hated Kalamainu'u, who once stole one of her husbands. That is how Puna paddled out with Kalamainu'u and survived to tell the story.

Opposite: Kūmimi Beach, Molokai

LEHUA

WAIKĪKĪ BEACH BOYS

Waikīkī is one of Hawai'i's most beloved wahi pana (a celebrated place). For countless generations, the royalty of O'ahu lived or sojourned at Helumoa, a massive coconut grove (ten thousand trees) that existed where the Royal Hawaiian Hotel and Shopping Center now stand.

It was once a wetland fed by streams and springs—hence its name, which means "spouting fresh water." Waikīkī's abundance of incredible surf breaks was a source of fun for people of all ages, and the coconut trees that lined its sandy shores provided shade, drink, and food.

In the 1860s, there was an influx of foreign visitors to the islands. When they visited Waikīkī, the sight of Hawaiians expertly navigating the surf with their bodies, boards, and canoes filled them with awe—as did the surfers' stunning physiques, a natural consequence of swimming and surfing their entire lives.

Despite the growing number of visitors between the 1860s and 1880s, it wasn't until 1901 that Waikīkī saw its first real hotel. Built on the stretch of shore known as Ulukou, the luxurious Moana Hotel had seventy-five rooms and offered upscale amenities. Its opening marked the beginning of Waikīkī tourism. Ulukou had a gentle surf break, perfect for tourists with little to no water skills to experience the ocean. Before long, Hawaiian youths were giving them surfing lessons and taking them surfing on outrigger canoes. This was the start of the Waikīkī beach boys, who forever shaped how the outside world thinks of surfing.

The beach boys relied on the generosity of wealthy visitors to make a living. Tourists might tip them with hard cash or take them out for drinks and dinner. Before long, their calling became a lifestyle. When the beach boys weren't giving lessons or surfing for their own enjoyment, they played ukuleles or

Top: Waikīkī, 1916

Bottom: Hui Nalu, 1919

Opposite, top: Waikīkī, 1908

Opposite, bottom: Waikīkī, 1927

guitars and sang to pass the time—much to tourists' joy.

In the early 1900s, two sports associations stepped in to guide and organize the beach boys—the Outrigger Canoe Club and the Hui Nalu Surf Club. The Outrigger was the first to form (1908) and began as a whites-only club. Founder Alexander Hume Ford leased an acre and a half of prime shoreline between the Seaside and Moana hotels to store their surfboards and outrigger canoes. The property faced some of Waikīkī's best surf breaks. Ford founded the club to "maintain and keep alive the Hawaiian sports of surfboarding and native canoeing," which he believed risked extinction. Despite the newspapers' claims that Ford "saved" surfing, it was the beach boys who taught many Outrigger members how to surf, and the club continued to rely on their services.

In 1911, in reaction to the Outrigger's exclusionary policies, Duke Kahanamoku founded Hui Nalu (wave/surf club). From the onset, the two clubs were fiercely competitive. Their rivalry (sometimes friendly, sometimes not) played out over canoe races and surf competitions and continues to this day.

In 1916, "beach boy" became a profession when Hui Nalu Captain Edward Kaleleihealani "Dude" Miller negotiated with the Moana to create a beach boy concession. They would offer swimming and surfing lessons and canoe rides, keep the beach safe and free of litter, and act as lifeguards. This crew was known as the Moana Bathhouse Gang.

Miller required them to be well-groomed and wear uniforms—scratchy black woolen bathing costumes that became heavy when wet and were totally unsuited for Hawai'i's climate and lifestyle. Despite this, Miller refused to let them roll down their costumes to be more comfortable.

In the mid-1920s, two companies collaborated to develop tourism even further. Castle & Cooke built the Royal Hawaiian, a luxury hotel at Helumoa, and Matson Navigation added more steamship routes to Hawai'i. When the

Brochure for the Oceanic Steamship Company, 1887

Moana Bathhouse Gang, 1918

hotel opened in 1927, it put Waikīkī on the map as an exclusive destination for the wealthy and the powerful. It also marked the beginning of the beach boys' heyday. Charismatic, athletic, and musical, they became as much of a tourist attraction as Waikīkī itself and acquired celebrity status. They were a unique institution—a combination of watermen, instructors, waiters, lifesavers, entertainers, and cultural ambassadors.

Waikīkī was their theater, and they acted the part of larger-than-life characters (because they were!). They gave themselves nicknames like Steamboat, Mystery, Panama, and Tarzan. Tourists could remember these more easily than Hawaiian names. These nicknames also defined their roles. The beach boys embodied the outside world's image of Hawai'i—an exotic place of permanent vacation where surfing, singing, and lounging on the beach was a way of life. This belied the true nature of surfing in Hawai'i. All Hawaiians surfed—farmers and fishers, old and young folk, and kings and queens—but for tourists, the glamorous, good-looking, life-is-a-party beach boys were their first vision of surfing, and this forever shaped the Western idea of surf culture. The tourist industry happily promoted that image on posters around the world.

Soon European royalty, Hollywood celebrities, international dignitaries, and wealthy heiresses wanted to meet Waikīkī beach boys.

Following, top left: Chick Daniels

Following, top right: Singer Ruth Etting attended to by Sally Hale and Sam Colgate

Following, bottom: Frank Sinatra and Ava Gardner go canoe-surfing with Captain Chas Lambert and Gene "Tarzan" Smith

WAIKIKI BEACH PATROL
O.C.C.

An editorial in *The Honolulu Advertiser* captures the extent to which the beach boys were an essential part of the Waikīkī experience:

> It is Sunday night, the night of expectation for tourists, for Sunday night after Sunday night for years the Hawaiian beach boys have assembled at the [Moana Hotel's] pier end, just for themselves, to sing and play as the urge impelled them to sing the songs of old Hawaii, the songs, many of them, that were the entrancing threads of life in Hawaii when Kalakaua was king and his islands a monarchy, songs that stirred the heart and often brought tears to the eyes.
>
> Hush, they've begun to sing. You hardly realize that melody is stirring; so soft, so murmuring is the deep strum of the guitar and the tinkle of the ukulele; as though they felt that the billows rolling in on the beach at Waikiki were rendering the diaphanous note. They sing softly, emotionally, their voices synchronizing—blending beautifully . . .
>
> Sing on Dave and Hiram and Bill and Sam, and all the boys of Waikiki Beach, the boys who are known around the world. Sing on, for then and only then do the travelers visiting in Hawaii realize that that is just a remnant of the picturesque old Hawaii.

Not to be outdone, the Royal Hawaiian hired beach boys to play music on weekday afternoons.

The beach boys were as much performers as they were watermen. In 1931, they hosted a comedy show for an athletic club banquet. In one skit, they competed in a "bathing beauty" contest. For another skit, they turned the stage into a beach complete with umbrellas to parody their jobs: beach talk, coconut oil rubdowns, and tourists' attempts to surf. During this time, the beach boys upped their service game by offering massages on the beach. These massages were not limited to male tourists. In the era of U.S. racial segregation, it was unheard of for brown men to publicly touch white American women.

In 1932, British actress Dorothy Mackaill, who vacationed often in Hawai'i, wrote a tell-all article about the romances between "rich American women" and beach boys. Mackaill noted: "These affairs have been invited by the white women visitors. The 'beach boys' have been spoiled by so many American women paying attention to them. By contrast, they are extremely deferential when put in their place." On the topic of massages, Mackaill opined, "It is little short of disgraceful to see how some white women lie on the beach at Waikiki in abbreviated bathing suits and permit the 'beach boys' to rub them with coconut oil so they will get a good tan." Perhaps decorum kept her from mentioning that the women would sometimes slip the beach boys their hotel room keys for later.

Previous, top: Outrigger Canoe Club Waikīkī Beach Patrol, 1935; (from left to right) Charles Baptiste, Harry Cornwale, Sam Kaluhiokalani, Joe Miner, Sally Hale, John Makua, Pua Kealoha, Chick Daniels, and Ted Waters

Previous, bottom right: Sam "Steamboat" Mokuahi

Opposite, top: Joe Miner provides lomi lomi in front of the Royal Hawaiian Hotel, 1936

Opposite, bottom: (from left to right) Duke Kahanamoku, unknown, Panama Dave, Joe Miner, Curly Cornwall, Charles Amalu, and Joe Guerro; 1934

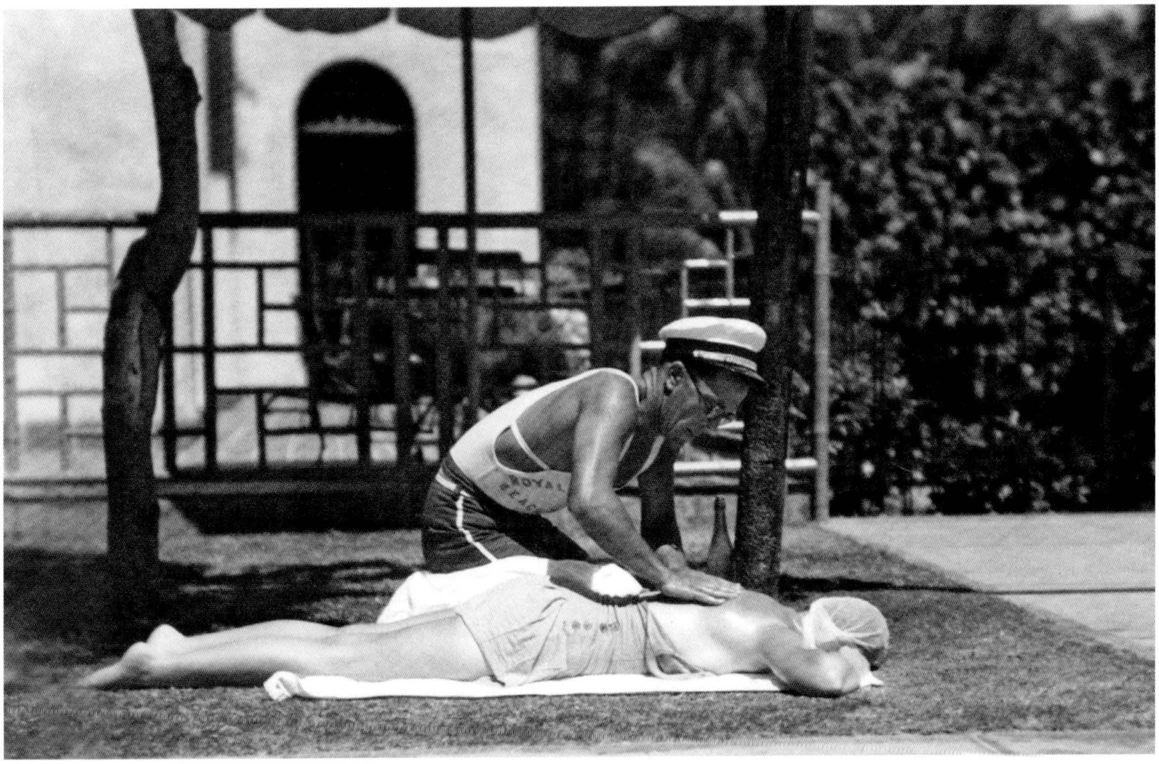
ROYAL

For many women, the highlight of their vacation was to be picked up by a beach boy. Circa 1950.

Despite the underlying racial tension that characterized that period, the beach boys became a beloved institution. During the mid to late 1930s, cultural organizations invited them to create and ride floats (complete with canoes and surfers on surfboards) for Kamehameha Day parades and participate in pageants dressed as ali'i and warriors of old. As tourism expanded to other islands like Maui, the idea of "beach boys" followed. Wherever hotels or tourists settled down, charming, good-looking, great-surfing men were there to help and to earn a very good living. Though they worked for tips, wealthy clientele made it worth their while. By 1937, members of the Waikīkī Beach Patrol were earning up to $300 a month during the high season, equal to about $6,600 today.

But the beach boys' heyday was about to end. On December 7, 1941, tourism stopped completely when the Japanese bombed Pearl Harbor. Once the war was over, tourism gradually returned to its prior levels, but its glamorous era came to a close. The beach boys' celebrity status may have waned, but they continue to be cultural bearers and ocean ambassadors.

As older generations of beach boys passed away, new generations of beach boys, including non-Hawaiians, stepped up to keep their legacy alive to this day.

JP Kaleopa'a, modern day beach boy

MORE GO
PROTEIN-RICH MILK

BOBBY AH CHOY

(1941–2007)

In 1957, a tsunami hit Honolulu, but the city buses gamely went about their routes, plowing through the flooded streets. As the buses drove past Waikīkī Beach, the wave they left in their wake caught the eye of three beach boys. Wherever there's a wave, beach boys see a challenge. One of them, sixteen-year-old Bobby Ah Choy, grabbed a board and surfed alongside the bus. A photojournalist for the *Honolulu Star-Advertiser,* Warren Roll, saw them having fun and snapped this classic image.

For fifty years, Bobby Ah Choy was an outrigger canoe captain and proud member of the Waikīkī beach boy tradition. Riding alongside a bus wasn't the last time he found unconventional ways to surf. When his friends bet he couldn't surf a door, he went home, took the door off his house, brought it to the ocean, and surfed with it (apparently his dad wasn't too pleased about the door's adventure). He was one of the original innovators of stand-up paddleboarding. Bobby and his brother Leroy began using stand-up paddleboards (SUPs), barely known in the 1960s, to carry cameras into the water for better photos. Since then, SUPs have exploded in popularity. When Bobby died, his ashes were scattered in the waters of Waikīkī.

ME'E NO HE'E NALU: Surfing Hero

DUKE KAHANAMOKU

(1890–1968)

Duke Paoa Kahanamoku is the most photographed and written-about Hawaiian in history. In 1999, *Surfer* magazine named him "The Surfer of the Century." But Duke never competed in surfing competitions. There are very few photos and, sadly, no footage of him surfing. His Olympic accomplishments came from swimming. What made Duke so influential was simple—he loved to surf. "Surfing," he said, "is the greatest thrill of my life." When he swam to international Olympic fame at the age of twenty-two, he traveled the world sharing this thrill with everyone he met.

Duke was born on August 24, 1890, in Honolulu. Before he even got his first wooden board, he pounded a kerosene can flat with a rock so he could catch waves with it. By the time he was a teenager, he'd developed board-making skills that would serve him his whole life: "There were none around Honolulu able to shape better than me." Lugging those heavy boards, which weighed 80 to 150 pounds, kept all the beach boys fit, but even in Waikīkī, Duke's athleticism stood out.

When Olympic officials came to Hawai'i scouting for swimmers, everyone encouraged Duke to try out. It was the first time he was timed on a 100-meter course . . . and he finished in 55.4 seconds, breaking the world's record by 4.6 seconds! This result was so unbelievable that Olympic officials made Duke come to the East Coast to replicate the feat, so he did, winning the U.S. time trials.

By the time he was selected for the 1912 Stockholm Olympics, the press was fascinated. Just fourteen years earlier, the U.S. had annexed Hawai'i as a territory, and Americans were curious about all things Hawaiian. Ukuleles arrived on the mainland that year, and then came Duke, looking like a tropical Greek god—six feet tall, 190 pounds, insanely fit, handsome (with world-class hair), emerging from the Pacific faster than anyone on Earth. It was the stuff of fiction.

OUT OF THE WATER, I AM NOTHING.

—DUKE KAHANAMOKU

Stockholm's newspapers were equally thrilled. Before Duke's arrival, they printed a photo of him "foam riding" shirtless, wildly risqué at the time. One reporter wrote: "[Duke was] the talk of the town today, not only for what he does, but for the easy, nonchalant way in which he does it." His laid-back attitude extended to training in the lead-up to the Games. Duke found "tank-swimming" joyless, so he took a wooden plank out onto the River Strom that cut through the city. When someone cried, "There's a Native sliding on the water!" traffic stopped, and crowds rushed the riverbank. Duke emerged dripping wet and grinning, handed the starstruck locals his board, and said, "Would you like to try surfing yourself?"

This combination of fame, showstopping exhibitions, easygoing charm, and generosity of spirit marked the beginning of Duke's career as the Johnny Appleseed of surfing. When he returned to America, crowds clamored to see the man who broke the world's record for the 100-meter course and won Olympic gold with ease (he was napping only minutes before the final). But what Duke really wanted to do was surf. His brother had shipped two surfboards from Honolulu, and Duke took them out to Rockaway Beach and Coney Island in New York. The crowds followed. He described the experience, "Cold was the word! . . . I caught a giant swell and roared in all the way to shore at express train speed. The throng on shore loved it." Then he surfed Atlantic City, New Jersey, and wrote to his father "having a great time . . . thousands of people were on the Million Dollar Pier." The next day, children returned to Atlantic City's beach with their mothers' ironing boards. The papers reported that "a new impetus has been given to surf riding and boys and men may be seen at any hour of the day . . . trying their skill striding in with the waves."

Following, bottom left: Hawaiian Olympic swimmers Harold Kruger, Clarence Lane, and Duke Kahanamoku perform for a Red Cross Benefit, Brighton Beach, Brooklyn, New York, 1918

For many years it has been a desire of mine to see people from other nations derive pleasure from the Hawaiian surfboard. Hawaiian surfriding reaches back in the ages of legends when our kings and chiefs found surfriding their favorite pastime, and surfriding has endured in Hawai'i through wars, plagues, and famine. . . . It is my dream to someday tour other countries and personally acquaint the people with the uses of the surfboard. For as an aid in life saving and physical development of boys and girls, it commands respect the world over.

—DUKE KAHANAMOKU

Wallen Retains National 880-Yd. Swimming Title

Chicago Star Defeats Lieut. Langer in Race at Pelham Bay

By A. C. Cavagnaro

William (Bud) Wallen, representing the Great Lakes Naval Training Station, of Chicago, stamped himself as an athlete worthy of possessing the 880-yard swimming championship in successfully defending his title in the annual competition, which was part of the water carnival at the Pelham Bay Naval Training Station yesterday.

Wallen was compelled to show his best speed in defeating Lieutenant Ludy Langer, of Camp Gordon, Georgia, by one yard in one of the most gruelling races on record. So bitter was the fight between the two men for the title that in crossing the finish line in 11 minutes 27 1-5 seconds Wallen established a new American record. The previous mark of 11:27 3-5 was to the credit of Norman Ross, of San Francisco, now in the aviation service, made in Honolulu Bay last September.

Harold E. Krueger, from Hawaii, finished third, almost fifty yards in the wake of Lieutenant Langer, while Leo Giebel, unattached, was fourth. Giebel killed his chance for the championship early in the race when he swam out of the course and before he could regain his tracks he had lost a margin of 100 yards.

Race Thrills Spectators

It was a thrill throughout for the spectators who witnessed Wallen and Lieutenant Langer fight their duel. Wallen, with a smooth and powerful trudgeon-crawl stroke, swept into the lead at the outset, and for the first lap had close company in his three other rivals. After turning the 110-yard stake, however, the race developed into a tussle between the defending champion and Lieutenant Langer.

Wallen held the fore position throughout the race, but at no time did he enjoy a comfortable margin over his soldier rival. The Chicago sailor scented the hard task in front of him. In taking the turns Lieutenant Langer had the advantage of his rival. Although Wallen would gain slightly on the run down to the next take-off float, Lieutenant Langer would shorten the gap at the turns.

Passing the 440-yard mark in 5:34 Wallen held an advantage of four yards, but he was using every ounce of speed to ward off his opponent. The final 220 yards found both men sprinting along at breakneck speed. Lieutenant Langer, who is known for his wonderful sprinting ability, came on strongly during the final fifty yards, and although he managed to get to Wallen's feet, he was never able to overtake him.

Kahanamoku Defeated

Duke P. Kahanamoku, the Hawaiian speed marvel, suffered his first defeat since his local invasion, but although beaten, he performed in a manner that was most astonishing. The Duke finished second in the 110-yard invitation handicap race, losing by one foot to Harold E. Krueger, another Hawaiian, who is touring the country with him. Kahanamoku strated from scratch and covered the distance in the remarkably fast time of 55 4-5 seconds.

Although there is no time on record for this distance, it was announced that these figures had never been approached in competition. It was the opinion among the spectators that the course was undoubtedly short, as the two floats that marked the distance were laid at low tide. Therefore, with the rising tide it was assumed that the floats had been pulled closer together.

Krueger had an eight-second allowance, while J. W. Newnon, Pelham Bay, the other starter, had fourteen seconds. Kahanamoku literally crawled up on his opponents by leaps and bounds, and at the 100-yard mark had passed Newnon and was within several yards of Krueger. The Duke never let up in his efforts and was practically at Kruger's side when the latter touched the finishing mark.

The third member of the visiting Honolulu party, Clarence E. Lane, also placed a victory to his credit. Lane started in the 110-yard handicap race and, although giving generous allowance to his rivals, won as he pleased.

The triple oar swim, indulged in by Lane, Krueger and Kahanamoku, gave the spectators an opportunity to see the wonderful swimming ability of the Hawaiians.

The summary follows:

880-yard national championship—Won by William Wallen, Great Lakes Naval Station; Lieutenant Ludy Langer, Camp Gordon, Ga., second; Harold E. Krueger, Honolulu, third; Leo Giebel, unattached, fourth. Time, 11:27 1-5.

100-yard breast stroke (closed to Pelham Bay)—Won by H. Oldaker, 3d Regiment; H. E. Shields, 1st Regiment, second; F. T. Lavery, 1st Regiment, third. Time, 1:55 4-5.

Duke Kahanamoku, Hawaiian Swimmer

THE famous water champion has been caught in action below by The Tribune's camera man. The centre picture (above) shows him at full speed with the "crawl stroke," while the three photographs below illustrate the use of the hands and legs in this method of swimming. On the left and right the Honolulan is posing for his picture and in the central oval his smile tells how fine is the water.

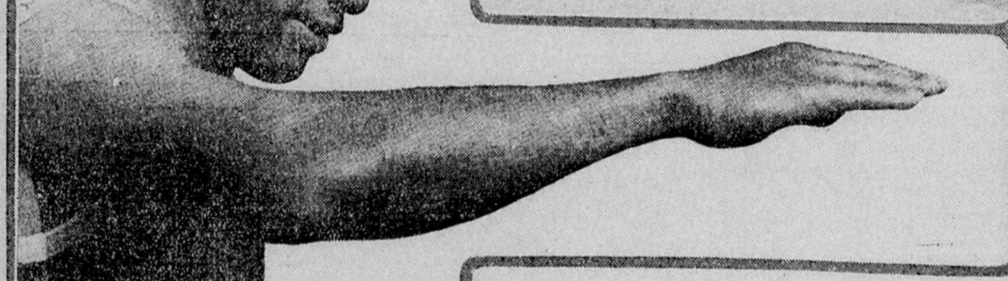

Title of Duke Merely Wished on Kahanamoku

Name Was Handed to Noted Swimmer by Some One in Hawaii

By Louis Lee Arms

Duke P. Kahanamoku, of Honolulu, isn't actually a duke as a surprising

power, but to our mind he is less graceful than some of the leading American swimmers. Kahanamoku is heavy-legged and heavy-chested, which gives him in the water less of the eel-like grace than is possessed by Ludy Langer, of Los Angeles, or Hal Vollmer, of New York.

Has Perfect Stroke

But mechanically Kahanamoku's stroke is perfection, with a conserva-

Pores, Ba
Old Forr
Three-M

Five-Mile Char
Handily at N
Weekly

A return to his ol
by Charles Pores, t
mile champion, in w
mile handicap run a
and field games of t
letic Club held at T
terday. Pores displa
speed and good judg
assumed the lead a
and won by 150 yar
Arthur Wilson, N
Club, and James W.
Athletic Club, who fi
third, respectively, v
ters for the greater
Pores came within
at one and a half
and Plant, speeding
managed to forge
Pores's consistent r
hauled them, and alt
fight for a short d
had to drop back.

White First in

A liberal handica
White, Salem-Cresc
in winning the 100-y
White had a start
this advantage prov
both Fred Teschner
who finished as na
Teschner was nosed
with Walters at the
though Walters had
he lost this ground
false start. This b
him first prize.
Joe McCabe, Pe
through in impress
the three-quarter-m
for enlisted men. M
running in the last
ning by several feet.

McKenna W

A new contender
ors came to light
Kenna, a student
won two races on
gramme. McKenna
and the manner in
his older opponent
able surprise to the
winning the 50-yard
good time of 26 4-5
ured the 100-yard h
ing from the 41-sec
The fancy dive
Saacke, a New Y
member, who had lit
feating the men tha
A four-oared shel
starters, was also sc
to the unfortunate
Major James A. McK
a member of the c
mittee, the event w
later date.
The summary foll

TRACK AN

100-yard dash (handi
J. White, Salem-Cresce
F. C. Teschner, Glenco
ond; P. K. Walters, Pa
third. Time, 0:10 3-5.
Three-mile run (
Charles Pores, Pelham
Wilson, New York A.
ond; J. W. Plant, Mo
yards), third. Time, 15
880-yard run (handic
Hill, unattached (40 ya
St. Christopher Club
Allan Mercer, New Yo
third. Time, 2:00 2-5.
Three-quarter mile r
ed men)—Won by Joe
(10 yards); J. Giorgi
yards), second; J. McA
yards), third. Time, 3:

SWIMM

100-yard swim (handi
McKenna, Fordham
F. W. Beggs, unattach
ond; L. P. Hansen, Y
onds), third. Time, 1:0
50-yard swim (novice
Kenna, Fordham Prep.
tached, second; E. S.
third. Time, 0:26 4-5.
Fancy dive (scratch
Saacke, New York A.
J. Henderson, unattach
second; J. J. O'Rourke,
points, third.
Four-oared rowing r
to the death in France
McKenna, Jr.

Brooklyn
Sets Tw
Field

This Hawaiian A Human Fish

Duke Kahanamoku, Who Made the Fastest Swimmers of the World Look Foolish at the Stockholm Olmypiad, Was Reared in the Surf of His Island Home and as a Boy Dodged Sharks for Sport.

By JIM NASIUM.

(Copyright by The Philadelphia Inquirer Co.)

THE Mermaid, being a poetic myth and a fictitious character of the artists' fevered imagination, the next nearest thing to a fish that masquerades in human form are the islanders of the Southern Pacific ocean, who can truthfully be said to be more at home in the water than on the land. [illegible]

[illegible]

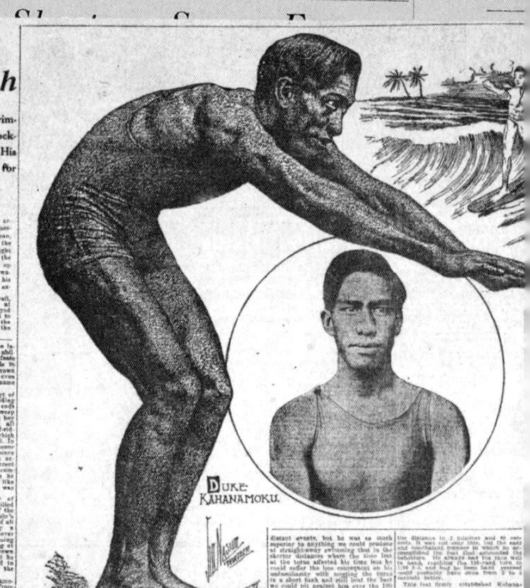

Promotional poster from Duke's tour of Australia, 1915

Despite his popularity, when the hoopla was over, Duke was stranded in New York, penniless, with no way to get home. Back in Honolulu, the Hui Nalu Club held fundraisers to pay his way, but this experience was a harbinger of what was to come. The dilemma of Olympic athletes in the amateur days was that earning money by competing made them "professional" and barred them from competing in the Olympics. Since Duke couldn't compete, he put on paid swimming exhibitions wherever he was invited, and wherever he swam, he surfed just for the thrill. That's how Duke began the travels that earned him the tag "the father of modern surfing."

In 1914, he traveled the coast of California—San Francisco, Santa Cruz, and Corona del Mar (where he surfed a quarter of a mile standing on his head). At that time, there were an estimated two hundred surfers in all of California. But a newspaper reported: "Whenever Duke appeared with his board a great crowd gathered on the beaches to marvel at the ease with which he stood upright and rode the bucking waves as skillfully as a cowboy rides a bronco. Everywhere he was besieged with pupils anxious to learn his methods." Duke inspired people to get into the ocean, leaving new surfers in his wake.

This was most evident in his trip to Australia. Australians knew him because of his Olympic win, but also because in Stockholm, he befriended the Australian team. His open, sharing nature prompted him to give them (his rivals!) a demonstration of his famous "Kahanamoku kick." Duke arrived in Sydney for a swimming exhibition, but they were just as eager to see him surf. Surfing existed in Australia, but only in the white water on crudely made boards.

Duke had no board, but when he remarked that he could make one, the news made the papers. Hawaiians were the most advanced board makers in the Pacific, and Duke was going to give a live demonstration. After a lumberyard cut the basic shape, Duke spent four days shaping the rail and bottom, "proving himself a fine craftsman." This was the first professionally shaped Hawaiian surfboard in Australia, and the Aussies treated it with reverence. The board got its own photo shoot on its travels to Sydney's Freshwater Beach, where posters advertised: "The famous swimmer will give an exhibition of breaker shooting and board shooting."

Duke didn't disappoint. In front of a huge crowd, he "plunged into the water, and continued to swim out until those watching from the beach wondered when he would stop." He caught an unbroken wave and surfed across its face. No one in Australia had seen anything like this. Then he stood on his head. He rotated the board 360 degrees. To demonstrate tandem surfing, he brought a white teenage girl out with him. In a country with a deep history of racism, a brown man touching a white girl was almost unheard of, but when he lifted her over his head, the crowd was too busy cheering to notice.

When the trip was over, he left the board behind for the Aussies to study and replicate. More important, he scattered the seeds of knowledge from a thousand years of Hawaiian surfing culture—where to paddle, what's possible on a wave, and how to have fun doing it. He left behind the thrill of he'e nalu. Australia still marks Duke's arrival as the moment their surfing culture began, and they honored him with a statue overlooking Freshwater Beach. After that trip, Duke visited New Zealand and did it all over again!

Unlike most Olympic athletes, Duke's fame didn't fade. The 1916 Olympic Games were canceled due to World War I, but Duke returned for the 1920 Olympics and won two gold medals for the 100-meter freestyle (breaking his own world record) and the 4 × 200 relay. He acted in movies. In 1925, he became a front-page hero all over again, when a boat capsized in twenty-foot waves off California's Newport Beach. By chance, Duke and three friends were there with their boards. They paddled through the huge surf and rescued thirteen people. The publicity inspired American lifeguards to incorporate boards into their standard equipment.

Duke and a very probably hungover Babe Ruth

Duke at Freshwater, Sydney, Australia

Waikīkī, 1929. Duke holds Jane Waite on his shoulders. A national magazine reprinted this photo with the caption: "A white girl riding with 'surf-board god.'" From the article's title, "A Paradise Gone Mad," it isn't hard to know what the editors thought of this image.

Duke and Tom Blake, 1935. From the nails on the sides of the board, you can tell that this is a lightweight hollow-body board, one of Blake's many inventions. Working together, these two men formed a pivot point in surfing history, from traditional board riding to the modern era of high-performance surfing.

Since Duke spread surfing around the world, it's fitting that there are statues of him in many places. This one is in Waikīkī but he is also honored in Freshwater, Australia, as well as Christchurch, New Zealand, and Huntington Beach, California.

Duke was a national icon, and for the rest of his life, people of all sorts—celebrities, presidents, tourists—wanted to meet him. This became such an established practice that later in his life, the state of Hawai'i gave him a salaried position as "Official Greeter." Unofficially, though, Duke was an ambassador for the ocean. It didn't matter who he met, because what Duke really wanted to do was go out on the water. If he met Babe Ruth that day, well then, that meant Babe Ruth was going surfing with him.

He didn't just give his attention to the rich and famous. He inspired generations of new surfers. Gerry Lopez said, "Duke used to hang on the beach with all of us kids during some of the events. He seemed larger than life, and he got a kick out of us. He was a big role model."

Duke's easygoing nature made him the perfect mentor. How else do you explain his meeting with Tom Blake, a young man who approached Duke one day and told him that they'd shaken hands in a Detroit movie theater years before and it inspired Tom to move to Hawai'i and dedicate his life to surfing? Most people would get a restraining order, but Duke welcomed him. Blake went on to become the most influential inventor in modern surfing. He invented skegs, lightweight boards, and the water camera, to name a few. But he did it working alongside Duke, who freely offered his acceptance, approval, and lifetime of knowledge.

Duke's main surfing advice was "Take your time—the wave comes. Let the other guys go; catch another one." Every surfer knows that can be the hardest advice to follow, but it comes from a mindset that's much deeper than surfing. Duke's philosophy was so simple that it fit on the back of the cards he handed out to the tens of thousands of people he met in his life:

ALOHA

In Hawai'i, we greet friends, loved ones and strangers with Aloha, which means with LOVE.

ALOHA is the key word to the universal spirit of real hospitality, which makes Hawai'i renowned as the world's center of understanding and fellowship. Try meeting or leaving people with ALOHA. You'll be surprised by their reaction. I believe it and it is my creed.

ALOHA to you.

—DUKE KAHANAMOKU

Opposite: When Duke Kahanamoku competed in the 1912 Olympics, he told reporters that he hoped surfing would one day be popular enough around the world to become an Olympic sport. In 2020, his wish came true and, fittingly, Hawaiian surfer Carissa Moore won gold in the women's division. This mural in downtown Honolulu by artist Kamea Hadar honors the connection between Hawai'i's past and present.

Below: Carissa Moore

KAHANAMOKU STRONG

Duke's accomplishments don't seem so outlandish when you know more about his family. His brother Sam was in the 1924 Paris Olympics along with him, and the Americans swept the 100-meter, with Duke in second, Sam in third, and Johnny Weissmuller (aka the man who played Tarzan) in first. Duke later joked: "It took Tarzan to finally beat me."

A story that has been lost in time, but deserves recognition, is about Duke's brother Sargent. On July 28, 1933, Sargent went out on a speedboat with a friend, but three and a half miles off Waikīkī, the engine died, and the boat started to drift. There was no paddle on the boat, so Sargent jumped in the ocean to tow it by himself. Because there was no rope, he grabbed the boat with one arm and paddled with the other. Four hours later, they made it safely to shore.

Kahanamoku Brothers (from left to right): Bill, Sam, Louis, David, Sargent, and Duke. 1931.

HAWAIIAN OLYMPIANS

In all the well-earned adulation of Duke Kahanamoku, what is often overlooked is that his presence at the 1912 Olympics opened the floodgates to the water talents of Hawaiians. By the 1920 Olympics, a large portion of the U.S. swim team came from Hawai'i. In the 100-meter freestyle, Duke took the gold, but silver and bronze went to Hawaiians as well. The three fastest swimmers in the world were Hawaiian.

They proved it beyond a shadow of a doubt by taking the gold medal (and setting a new world record) in the 200-meter team relay. The silver medalist, Pua Kealoha (1902–1989), may have lost out on gold to Duke, but he established his own legendary status on his return to Hawai'i. He is said to be the first man to swim the Kaiwi Channel from Molokai to O'ahu, twenty-six miles (!) across shark-infested open ocean that is widely regarded as one of the most difficult swims on the planet. As of 2023, only a hundred people have matched the feat.

Pua's brother, Warren Kealoha, was no slouch, either. He spent six years as the world champion, world-record holder, and gold medalist in the backstroke. For decades afterward, the United States Olympic team wasn't complete without swimmers from Hawai'i.

Hawai'i swimmers at the 1924 Olympics in Paris. Front: Sam Kahanamoku, Charlie Pung, Mariechen Wehselau, Pua Kealoha. Back: Henry Luning, Bill Kirschbaum, Duke Kahanamoku, Warren Kealoha, William Harris, David Kahanamoku.

Charles Kauha in Waikīkī, 1893. Photographed right at the dawn of Western tourism, Kauha was considered to be one of the very first beach boys. This photo of him holding an alai'a became a popular postcard at the time, which spread this image around the world. It is now considered one of the most iconic photos in surfing history.

Daniel Keliihoomalu Kahala Jr. in Waikīkī, 2025

PART 4

HE‘E NALU TODAY

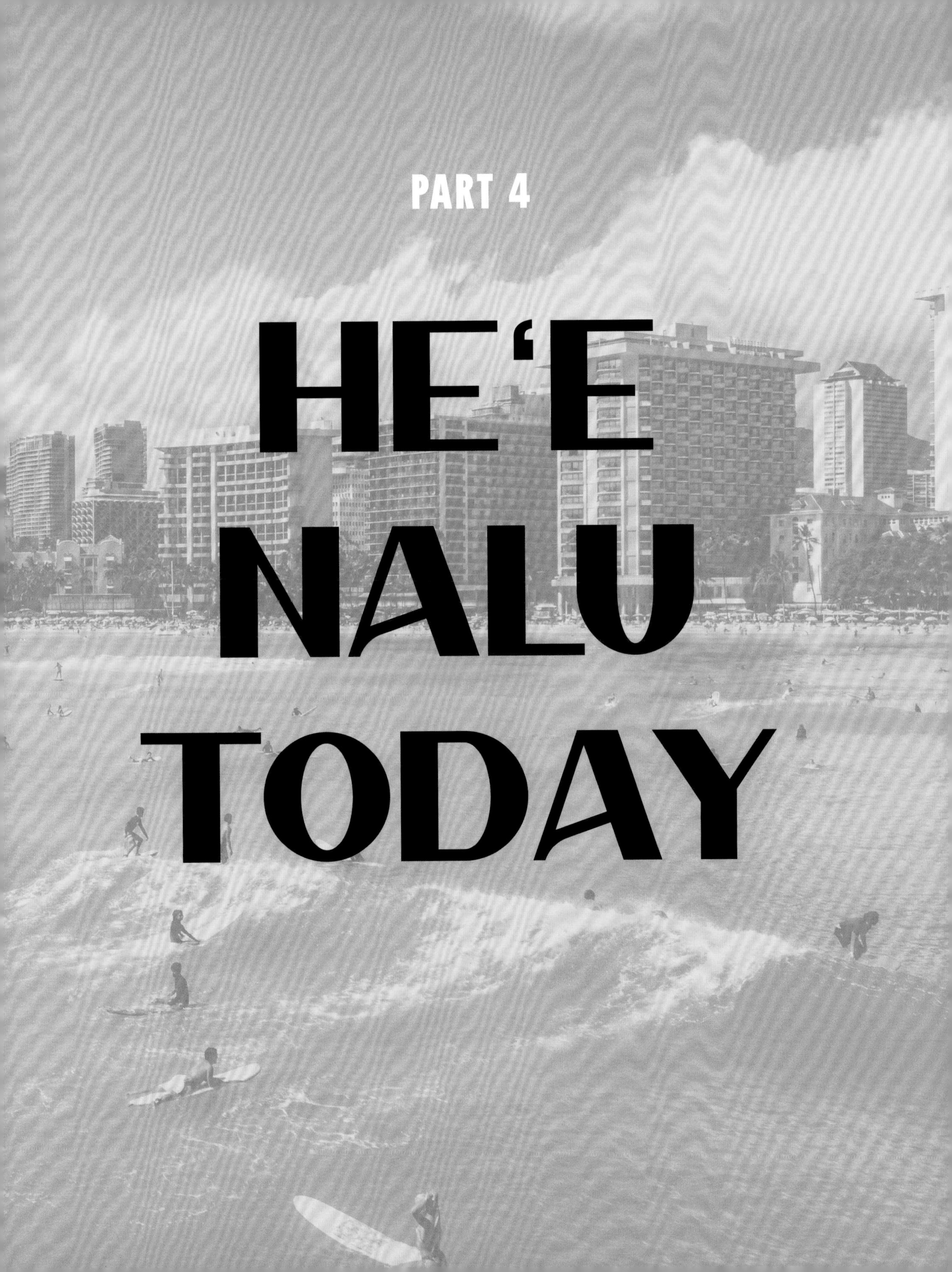

THE REBIRTH OF HAWAIIAN MASTER NAVIGATORS

KAHOʻOLAWE AND *HŌKŪLEʻA*

Imagine growing up hearing that your culture was a relic of the past. From the moment the first American Protestant missionaries arrived on Hawai'i's shores in 1820, they subjected Hawaiians to a litany of their failings as a people. Imagine more foreigners arriving every year, adding their voices to the barrage of criticism and bringing diseases that kill your people. Imagine your pain on January 17, 1893, when missionary descendants and white businessmen overthrew your kingdom, then replaced the Hawaiian language with English in schools. In 1900, these same people convinced the United States to annex Hawai'i as a territory. By 1948, the last Hawaiian language newspaper closed its doors. On August 16, 1959, your homeland became America's fiftieth state. Your language, land, and cultural practices were near extinction. This was the experience of the Hawaiian people.

And then—everything changed. Hawai'i's statehood coincided with the civil rights movement, which inspired Hawaiians to reestablish their identity as a people and reclaim their language and cultural practices.

Two significant events in the mid-1970s helped propel this movement forward. What tied them together is the ocean. Because Kanaloa personifies the ocean, ocean currents, and ocean winds, Hawaiians associate him with voyaging. Hawaiians consider the sacred island of Kaho'olawe to be one of the most important embodiments of Kanaloa. It is where ancient Hawaiian master navigators learned the art of wayfinding.

Above, right: A rain shrine on Kao'olawe dedicated to Kāne and Kamohoali'i (shark god and Pele's brother)

But in 1941, the United States began using the island for bombing practice. The bombing was so extensive that it broke the water table. On January 4, 1976, nine activists, who called themselves Protect Kaho'olawe 'Ohana (PKO), risked their lives by landing on the island to protest. Kaho'olawe was riddled with unexploded ordinance. A single wrong step could maim or kill them.

This was the first of several landings. Later, two core activists, George Helm and Kimo Mitchell, were lost at sea while paddling back to Maui from Kaho'olawe on surfboards. Because of PKO's efforts, including a federal lawsuit, bombing ended in 1990. People can now access the island under the supervision of trained leaders for "religious, cultural, educational, and scientific activities."

Ancient Hawaiian master navigators chose Kaho'olawe as the center of voyaging practices because the channel of Kealaikahiki (the path to Kahiki), between Kaho'olawe and Lāna'i, is the sea road that voyagers used to travel between Hawai'i and Kahiki. *Kahiki* is Hawaiian for *Tahiti,* but it also refers to any land beyond the Hawaiian Islands. There are many mytho-histories about seafaring cultural heroes voyaging between Hawai'i and Kahiki.

For unknown reasons, these voyages stopped between the fourteenth and fifteenth centuries—a mystery that has puzzled scholars. When the first Europeans stumbled across the Hawaiian Islands, they came up with their own explanation. It never happened. To the Western way of thinking, travel across the vast Pacific without a compass, sextant, and map simply wasn't possible. Hawai'i is the most remote place on earth, so the Polynesians' arrival there had to be as accidental

Big aloha welcomes Hokule'a

By ROBERT HOLLIS
Advertiser Staff Writer

Under showers of flowers, kisses and hugs from long-separated families and friends, the Polynesian canoe Hokule'a and its crew of 14 returned to Honolulu yesterday after its second 6,000-mile roundtrip voyage to Tahiti.

More than 500 well-wishers crowded the shoreline at Magic Island under occasionally showery skies as the 60-foot, double-hulled canoe docked at 1:05 p.m. accompanied by a flotilla of 30 pleasure craft and a Coast Guard escort.

While Gov. Ariyoshi and Mayor Fasi looked on, scores of long-separated loved ones clambered aboard the Hokule'a to embrace crew members, most of whom were deeply tanned after 22 days at sea.

"I'm a little lost," said Charles Nainoa Thompson, the 27-year-old part-Hawaiian navigator who successfully guided the canoe to the Society Islands and back, using only traditional methods of plotting the ship's position and course.

"I didn't expect all this," he added as he walked slowly through the cheering crowd while leis and kisses were showered on him.

The vessel and its crew were reported fit following the "really fast" return trip from Tahiti that began May 13, said Hokule'a skipper Gordon Pilanaia.

"The trip down was a lot longer," he added. "The trip home was just a nice sweet sail."

Most crew members described the

See HOKULE'A on Page A-3

The 60-foot Polynesian voyaging canoe Hokule'a is pulled into its Magic Island berth at the end of a rope.

as their own—surely they had been blown off course by a storm or pulled by a current. Ironically, in 1000 BCE, while Polynesians were navigating the ocean, the ancestors of those English explorers were still land-bound hunter-gatherers.

"Accidental discovery" was the dominant theory among historians and anthropologists for decades until the Polynesian Voyaging Society (PVS) proved them wrong. Ben Finney, an anthropologist specializing in the history of surfing; Herb Kawainui Kāne, a gifted artist and sailing enthusiast; and Tommy Holmes, a famous waterman and authority on Hawaiian canoes, formed the society in 1973 to research, revive, and perpetuate Polynesian voyaging. They decided to build and sail a double-hulled voyaging canoe and sail it from Hawai'i to Tahiti to prove that wayfinders intentionally settled the farthest reaches of Polynesia.

By 1975, they finished the canoe. It had two masts and was twenty feet wide and sixty-two feet long. They named it *Hōkūle'a* (Star of Gladness, known elsewhere as Arcturus), for the Hawaiian zenith star. Wayfinders use zenith stars to determine latitude and longitude in celestial navigation. The *Hōkūle'a* was an immediate sensation. Competition to be a crew member was fierce. The big-wave surfers of Waimea felt they were shoo-ins, but the Polynesian Voyaging Society considered them "shallow-water men." The *Hōkūle'a* needed deep-sea men, but most of all, it needed a master navigator. Unfortunately, in Hawai'i, the knowledge of open ocean navigation had been lost.

The PVS found who they were looking for in Satawal, an atoll in the Federated States of Micronesia. Master navigator Pius "Mau" Piailug agreed to guide the *Hōkūle'a* and to retrain Hawaiians in the art of voyaging. His first apprentice was the twenty-three-year-old Nainoa Thompson, the son of a former Waikīkī beach boy and Hui Nalu member, Myron "Pinkie" Thompson. Even the Bishop Museum pitched in to the effort by allowing Nainoa to stay overnight in their planetarium. They projected the night skies he would encounter along the route, so he could memorize them.

Following: The *Hōkūle'a* visiting the Buffalo Big Board Classic during the opening ceremony, 2025

Over a thousand people watched the *Hōkūle'a*'s dedication ceremony at Kāne'ohe Bay, O'ahu. Famed chanter Ka'upena Wong blessed the canoe, and then hundreds of spectators joined in to haul it into the ocean. Over the next year, the

TOLD THEIR GODS WERE FALSE, THEIR RITUALS FOOLISH, THEIR DRESS, DANCES, AND MANNERS UNACCEPTABLE, THEIR SKILLS AND TALENTS UNIMPORTANT, THE HAWAIIANS AS A PEOPLE KNEW AN "IDENTITY CRISIS" LONG BEFORE THE PHRASE WAS COINED.

—MARY KAWENA PUKUI

Hōkūle'a sailed around the islands to give the crew experience at sea. The sight of the *Hōkūle'a* was a reminder of a rich heritage and a symbol of hope. Crew member Billy Richards recalled, "Hawaiian families would picnic and spend a whole day at the beach just to stare at the canoe."

On May 1, 1976, hundreds of people lined the coast to watch the *Hōkūle'a* depart through the Kealaikahiki Channel, the sea road of their ancestors. It crossed 2,500 miles of the Pacific Ocean using only traditional wayfinding methods, although the trip had a distinctly Hawaiian touch. Once the steersman, Buffalo Keaulana, got a feel for the boat, he started catching so many waves that Mau had to reprimand him to stay on course.

On June 4, the *Hōkūle'a* arrived in Pape'ete Harbor, where half of Tahiti's population, more than seventeen thousand people, waited to greet them. Its arrival sparked immediate celebrations back in Hawai'i. The news was on television, in classrooms, and at every dinner table. The *Hōkūle'a* was to Polynesians what the 1969 moon landing was to Americans—an affirmation of an entire culture's knowledge and endeavors.

In 2025, on the fiftieth anniversary of the *Hōkūle'a*, Nainoa Thompson summed up its legacy:

> In 1973 there were no Polynesian voyaging canoes; today there are six with others under construction. In 1973 there was only one deep-sea navigator that PVS knew of; today there are nine, with several more in training, along with 135 experienced deep-sea sailors in Hawai'i alone ensuring that the Hawaiian people will never again lose their traditions of voyaging and navigation. Over the last 25 years, the family of the voyaging canoe has grown to more than 525,000 men, women, and children.

The return of Kaho'olawe and the *Hōkūle'a*'s voyages helped a resilient nation come back from the brink of cultural extinction. The 1980s saw the birth of Hawaiian language immersion schools. In 1993, thousands marched to mark the hundredth anniversary of the overthrow. Since then, several generations have grown up secure in their identity—speaking their language, valuing their knowledge, and proud of their heritage.

Hokule'a

BUFFALO'S BIG BOARD SURFING CLASSIC

How do you give back to the ocean after the ocean has given you everything?

Hōkūle'a steersman Richard Keaulana was born in 1935 and earned the nickname Buffalo when he was a child. He spent so much time in the water that his mother compared him to a water buffalo.

The ocean gave him work and companionship. His father died in an accident while saving others (saving people became a common trait for the Keaulanas). After that, Buffalo had to help support his family. He became a Waikīkī beach boy, then later, he moved to Mākaha. But on days when tourists in Waikīkī were scarce, the friends he'd made as a beach boy, like the legendary Rabbit Kekai, would load a truck full of boards and make a pilgrimage to see Buffalo and ride Mākaha's world-class surf alongside him. Buffalo grew to love Mākaha and saved so many lives that when lifeguarding became an official position, he was the only man considered for the job.

The ocean gave him a home. He often slept on the beach as a youth. When he became caretaker, he built a shelter on the shore and raised his family there. After he saved a Texas oilman from drowning in Mākaha's powerful surf, that man helped him buy a house.

The ocean fed him. His longtime friend, canoemate, and unofficial biographer, Bunky Bakutis, said, "If Buffalo had his speargun, you should start gathering wood, because you'd be cooking soon." As a kid with no lunch money, Buffalo would bring his

Opposite: Buffalo Keaulana in his prime.

speargun to school and dive for his lunch. As an adult, he and his wife, Leimomi, were known for looking after troubled kids in Mākaha, giving them food and aloha.

But most of all, the ocean gave him joy. His massive strength combined with grace in the water to make him one of the great surfers of the twentieth century. Before O'ahu's North Shore became the proving ground for the world's surf community, Mākaha was the place to make your name, and Buffalo knew those waters better than anyone.

In 1953, Mākaha was the site of the world's first international surfing competition. Buffalo won the bodysurfing division four times. He would've won more, but he had to pause for a few years (like Elvis) to serve in the military. The army made him a lifeguard, of course. When he came back in 1960, he won the longboarding competition.

Clarence Maki

Richard (Buffalo) Keaulana (left) and Henry Preece of Makaha Surf Club are ready for competition in the International Surf Championships.

Surf Meet Opens Today

Buffalo became so well-respected that in 1976, he was an obvious choice to be a crew member for the *Hōkūle'a*'s maiden voyage and became main steersman. Those weeks spent out on the open ocean, re-creating and remembering the craft and knowledge of their kūpuna, had a spiritual effect on the crew. "*Hōkūle'a* was a cultural reawakening for Buffalo on a personal level," said Bunky. Buffalo's life and talents were not an accident. They were a cultural treasure, an inheritance from thousands of years of oceangoing people. So what do you do with an inheritance? You pass it on.

In 1977, a year after Buffalo returned from Tahiti, he started the Buffalo Big Board Surfing Classic with the help of his wife and friends. This was not an international tournament where outsiders made the rules and acted as judges. Why should he let others tell him what good surfing is? This was Mākaha! People there play by their own rules. Back in the day, when they didn't have wood for surfboards, they pulled up

> I'M GOING TO CHANGE MY EVIL WAYS. FROM NOW ON, INSTEAD OF SPENDING MY LIFE DOING NOTHING BUT SURFING, DRINKING, AND SMOKING, I'M GOING TO START SAILING, DRINKING, AND SMOKING.
>
> —BUFFALO KEAULANA, AFTER RETURNING FROM HIS *HŌKŪLE'A* VOYAGE

railroad ties and used those. Mākaha means "fierce," and its people always maintained that reputation.

From the start, the Buffalo Big Board Classic has not been your average surf competition. It includes a category for surfers who weigh 250 or more pounds (weigh-in required). Bunky said, "In the first longboard competition, there were seven competitors, and they declared seven winners." And just in case anyone takes the contest too seriously, the scoring isn't based on the monotony of cutbacks, carves, and barrels that define professional surfing. Instead, Buffalo and his friends came up with their own far more entertaining scoring system.

You are rewarded for changing positions on the longboard as often as possible. Buffalo and his friends chose the positions, and they clearly enjoyed themselves—there's the "Buddha," the "Coffin" (like a corpse), the "Tiki," and more.

The "Dead Cockroach" is a particular favorite for anyone who grew up in Mākaha (like coauthor Alohalani), where you get dive bombed by cockroaches so big they're nicknamed B-52s. Most competitors do that pose at the end of the ride, because as funny as it is (it always makes the crowd laugh), riding a six-foot wave while backward and upside down is WAY harder than it looks.

The event's organization is just as loose. Forget following a schedule. Events are announced on the fly when the organizers are pretty sure all the competitors are there. If an event is announced and someone doesn't have their board, no problem. Someone is sure to lend them one. "The main thing is having fun," said Bunky. "The family aspect of it is the reason it's coming up on fifty years. I don't think there's an older surf meet in the world."

BUFFALO BIG BOARD CLASSIC 2025

The Buffalo (as it's known) is like an ocean rodeo combined with a two-weekend-long tailgate party on one of the best beaches in the world. Families bring tents and cots, guitars and grills. Laughter, music, and the smell of grilled meat drifts over the beach. This is tailgating at its finest. Many people live nearby, but some still sleep there overnight for the chance to be closer to the ocean. Families bring inflatable wading pools for children who are too little to play in the waves. If a family friend is driving a Jet Ski with the safety crew, they might roar over, decelerating at the exact right moment to gently swing the safety board around so your kid can climb aboard and go for a ride.

You won't find better Jet Ski drivers on the planet than the Mākaha crew that patrols this competition. One of Buffalo's sons, Brian, helped innovate their use for water rescue. He now advises the U.S. military and lifeguard organizations around the world. He handpicked and trained his water safety crew, and they're as much a part of the show as the surfers.

The safety crew keeps busy. The point break of Mākaha is so good that waves arrive almost nonstop. There's so much continuous action over the course of the two weekends that the surfing becomes part of the scenery and people pass the time cooking, drinking, and talking story with friends. But at the same time, everyone here is trained from birth to always keep one eye on the ocean. When a larger set appears on the horizon, everyone's attention instantly pivots to the water because they know the real show is about to begin.

The people on boards catch the waves easily, but getting a six-man canoe on a wave is a slightly harder feat. The crews paddle hard and the crowd groans in sympathy if they miss it, but cheer when they make the drop. On bigger waves, a crew member might climb out onto the ama (outrigger) to improve the canoe's balance and enjoy a spectacular ride. As the canoes race through the surf, it's a reminder that Hawaiians have been doing this for over a thousand years and they've gotten pretty damn good at it. If a canoe capsizes, Jet Skis swarm in, perfectly in sync and parallel with the set, to make the rescue before the next wave breaks.

This easy mixture of the old and the new makes this competition especially compelling. Some surfers ride the same style of wooden boards their ancestors used, while drones fly overhead, recording every move. During the 2025 opening ceremony, a chanter intoned a prayer to the gods while a car drove by blasting hip-hop. At dawn, the ultimate symbol of the continuity between past and present in Hawai'i sailed into view—the *Hōkūle'a* and its crew came to honor Buffalo.

This year's event was particularly special. Buffalo turned ninety. He'd been battling illness for a while, and the hospital released him just in time for the opening ceremony. The safety crew put him on a Jet Ski with Brian and a grandson, and together they rode out to greet the *Hōkūle'a*. This gesture of aloha

Opposite, top: Buffalo and Brian Keaulana ride out to meet the *Hōkūle'a*

Opposite, bottom right: Kaipo Cornwell being pulled to safety after a canoe capsized

Opposite, bottom left: Lyon Tang, Liloa Stowell, Cromwell Day, and Leon Mosher (steersman)

Following: A family competing on the supsquatch, a giant inflatable paddleboard that can hold 4 to 8 people. Teams are scored on the quality of their ride, the number of times they can spin the supsquatch 360 degrees, the level of awesomeness in their pose as they reach the shore, and who has the most fun.

XCEL
SCUBAPRO

OCEAN SAFETY

Noa Pu'u

between past and present *Hōkūle'a* crew members speaks to the way that Hawaiians pass their 'ike kai to the next generation—the true value of this competition.

When the ocean has been your livelihood, your grocery store, your playground, your gym, and your longest love affair, how do you return that favor? You pass it on. After a lifetime caring for its shores, this contest is Buffalo's way of looking after Mākaha even after he's gone. Mākaha suffers from poverty and all the ills that poverty brings, but its surf and beauty make it one of the wealthiest places on earth. "If you're busy all the time," Buffalo told coauthor Lendler, "you'll miss out on fishing and sailing and everything the ocean has to offer. You'll miss all of it."

Gathering people together to enjoy the ocean for two weekends a year is a reminder of what truly matters. This is an event where families are born. On the second Saturday in 2025, after the contest was done for that day, the announcer got married on the beach. This is an event that strengthens community ties through generosity. Winners received boards, and some gave them away to friends who were in need.

Once the competition ends, tents will come down, the beach will be swept clean, but the waves will keep breaking. The next day, a parent may bring their child out on a board. Together, they will enjoy the inheritance they've received from their kūpuna and the 'āina. Each generation will pass that joy down to the next generation and the next, one after another, just like waves in the ocean.

Micah DeSoto and his son Kea'aukapu DeSoto paddling out at their home break, Mākaha, O'ahu

LIFEGUARDS

In 2023, Luke Shepardson was scheduled to work his regular shift as a lifeguard on the North Shore. By coincidence, The Eddie surfing competition (page 267) was called that same day, and Luke was invited to compete. Luke's boss allowed him a break in his shift so he could go up against the most famous professional big-wave riders in the world. These were the people he spent his working hours protecting. Several hours later, Luke beat them all.

It was such a good underdog story (man wins big-wave contest on his coffee break) that it made news around the world. What did not make the news was this—that same day, North Shore lifeguards (including Luke) made 10,505 preventive actions (their term for telling people "You should *not* stand that close to the water") and sixty-four rescues, including saving a baby who got swept under a house! The difference in those numbers is the difference between what most people see (the waves in front of them) and what the lifeguards know (the waves that will come). That day, the lifeguards showed that they are as good as anyone on the waves, but they also possess the foresight that comes with ʻike kai—knowledge of the sea.

"We're not in the hero business," says Mark Cunningham, one of the longest-serving lifeguards on the North Shore. "Every time we have to make a rescue, we feel like we let the situation get too far—we should have seen it coming."

Lifeguards are the unsung heroes of Hawaiʻi, but they are not *just* first responders in the ocean. They are bearers of cultural knowledge, passing down the water knowledge of an entire people. Hawaiians are rightly celebrated for their contributions to surfing, but they have been just as influential in water safety.

The ocean provides me with knowledge, skill, and opportunity to see the outcome before it happens so I may decide where and when to be. To coexist between calm and chaos. To never have fear.

—BRIAN KEAULANA,
LEGENDARY LIFEGUARD AND BIG-WAVE SURFER

In the early 1900s, George Freeth introduced surfing to Southern California, and when he became a lifeguard at Venice Beach, he innovated the idea of using the board for rescue. In the 1980s, surfer/lifeguards Brian Keaulana, Melvin Pu'u, Terry Ahue, and Dennis Gouveia began experimenting with Jet Skis in their work. These are now-standard equipment for lifeguards around the world.

The ocean can kill you in so many ways that water safety is a natural part of water culture. However, the need for someone to dedicate their time to water safety intensified in Hawai'i with the arrival of foreigners. At the beginning of the twentieth century, the Waikīkī beach boys faced an unexpected challenge. Their ease in the ocean and the beauty of Waikīkī attracted tourists who couldn't swim well. This was a novel concept in Hawai'i, where everyone grew up in the ocean. Tourist rescue became a regular part of the beach boys' duties. But as more people arrived, the demands for lifesaving increased. As one newspaper in 1917 lamented, "The Outrigger Club has once again come to the assistance of those who are weak swimmers."

That year, Hawai'i established a full-time "Life-Saving Patrol" for Waikīkī Beach. The first lifeguards were two men "selected for their strength and ability as swimmers and boatmen." One of those men was Duke Kahanamoku's brother, David, a beach boy whom many reckoned was a better surfer than Duke himself. From that moment, the lifeguard service has evolved in a similar pattern. In every location, there were locals who knew its every current, tide, and season and were saving people long before "lifeguard" became a profession.

The North Shore is a perfect example. The early big-wave surfers of Pipeline and Waimea in the 1950s and '60s spent as much time saving lives as surfing. An unexpected side effect of going out in heavy surf was that it inspired amateurs—like members of the U.S. military stationed in Hawai'i—to try it, too. Water rescue was officially the job of the North Shore's fire department, but they were overwhelmed by what were sometimes dozens of rescues a day. Plus, as one fireman in 1967 put it, "Yes, we need lifeguards at Waimea Bay during the winter, but you'd have to find a crazy man to take the job. That's a wild place."

The answer was to appoint the crazy people who were already voluntarily spending their time in the ocean. Former Honolulu Ocean Safety Chief Jim Howe said, "Here in Hawai'i, the lifeguarding service really is the surfing community. We wanted to hire surfers because we need people who understand the ocean and are not afraid of it."

Knowledge of the ocean requires the ability to move well in it, and the physical abilities of Hawai'i's lifeguards have never been in doubt. In 1950, William Melvin Smith Jr., who was half Irish and half Hawaiian, was named the first captain of the lifeguard service. Just two years earlier, he became one of the greatest swimmers of the twentieth century when he won two Olympic gold medals, set seven world records, and eighteen American records. Over his twenty-five-year

WHATEVER MOTHER NATURE HAS IN STORE FOR YOU THAT DAY IS WHAT YOU'RE DOING.

—KA'AUMOANA DAVIS, LIFEGUARD

Opposite, top left: Tourist brochure for the many services provided by the Waikīkī Beach Patrol: "You can rely on them, secure in the knowledge that they are gentlemen . . . "

Opposite, top right: Captain Sally Hale, Waikīkī Beach Patrol headquarters. This hut served as the first official lifeguard station.

Opposite, bottom: Outrigger Canoe Club Waikīkī Beach Patrol, 1935

Surfing
AND BEACH SPORTS AT WAIKIKI
UNDER THE COMPETENT AND SKILLED DIRECTION OF THE WAIKIKI BEACH PATROL
WAIKIKI BEACH PATROL
O.C.C.

WAIKIKI BEACH PATROL
CANOE SURFING
SURFBOARDS
Beach Umbrellas
Swimming & Surfing INSTRUCTION
Moonlight Canoe PARTIES
Picture Taking
Glass Box PARTIES
HEADQUARTERS
To Dick -
In memory of happy
hours at Waikiki Beach.
Aloha Nui

career, as the service expanded from six people watching over Waikīkī to two hundred stationed all around Oʻahu, he handpicked each lifeguard. Hawaiʻi's lifeguards have included Olympic medalists, state and college swimming champions, and professional surfers.

They have to be good. When big swells come to the islands it can catch everyone (except the lifeguards) by surprise. In the summer of 2022, lifeguards made 2,105 rescues in *one weekend*. And they do it all for some of the lowest wages of any first responders in Hawaiʻi. In 2024, lifeguards made approximately $21 an hour. Lifeguard Kaʻaumoana Davis says, "We're always putting ourselves in situations where conditions are extreme or unsafe. . . . We have to trust our instincts, knowledge of the ocean, the current, the beach, and our physical capabilities, all while attempting to save someone's life—more often than not, a complete stranger."

With such little fiscal reward, what motivates lifeguards to accept such a demanding task? Cunningham says it's simple. Lifeguards are "fit and strong and stoked and helping people and having a good time in the ocean and getting paid for going to the beach."

YOU HAVE TO HAVE THE BEST KNOWLEDGE AND SKILL THERE IS TO WORK AT WAIMEA. NOT JUST BETTER THAN AVERAGE, OR SUPERIOR, BUT THE BEST.

—EDDIE AIKAU

Lifeguards (from left to right) Cody Kauha'aha'a, Tony, and JoJo watching over Point surf break, Ho'okipa, Maui

Luke Shepardson's winning ride at
The Eddie in 2023, Waimea Bay, O'ahu

MEʻE NO HEʻE NALU: Surfing Hero

RELL SUNN

(1950–1998)

When Rell Sunn paddled into a lineup, she brightened everyone's day. She would slip off her board and swim around to hug and kiss friends. She would joke, give kids advice, and reprimand wave hogs—even the stone-cold guys everyone was scared of. "For every one wave you catch, you have to let three go by," she would say. "You got to share." She was such a talker that the local radio station hired her to give the daily surf report. Her signature line became, "Surf's up. No need to go to school today." When told this might not be the best advice for kids, she replied: "Well, there's lessons out there in the waves, too."

Rell Sunn isn't as well-known outside Hawaiʻi as her male contemporaries like Gerry Lopez and Eddie Aikau. But to those who knew her, Rell epitomized Hawaiʻi. Before Rell's birth, her grandmother dreamed that her middle name should be Kapolioka'ehukai (heart of the sea). On July 31, 1950, she was born Roella Kapolioka'ehukai Sunn. Her grandmother proved to be prophetic. Rell took to the ocean right away.

Kapolioka'ehukai wasn't Rell's only name that proved apt. Up through high school, people called her Rella Propella. She didn't love that name, but it stuck because it described her boundless energy in the ocean. At age fourteen, "I won my first surfboard. . . . I slept with it for about two weeks, I think. It was my best friend." As good a surfer as she was, she was even better at free-diving and spearfishing.

Men in Mākaha, no slouches in the water themselves, knew that if their spear fell to the ocean floor beyond their reach, Rell could get it . . . then resurface and announce, "You owe me lunch."

At that time, if you were a male hotshot surfer, you could go pro and earn a living. If you were a woman, there was nothing. After community college, Rell got married, moved to Oklahoma, and had a daughter. A few years later, the marriage ended, and she brought her daughter back to Mākaha, where she stayed the rest of her life, rooted.

These were the years she earned her new nickname: the Queen of Mākaha. Like a queen, she was beloved. One of her role models was Duke Kahanamoku, with his regal combination of athleticism and aloha. Her grace on the waves reminded many of the hula that she and her sisters loved. On the North Shore, she braved heavy surf alongside men. On the South Shore, she brought Chinese takeout to Waikīkī lifeguards to thank them. She organized moonlight surf sessions, with glow sticks for better party vibes (and safety, too).

On the West Shore . . . well, she *was* Mākaha. Beautiful and fierce. She never lacked for suitors. Surfers and photographers were smitten with her. But she also had a black belt in judo and the iron will required to be a single mother. Jeff Divine, renowned surf photographer and longtime boyfriend of Rell, said, "It took a lot to set her off. But actually, she could be a real badass, and she got nothing but respect for it . . . She'd rip your eyes out if she had to."

That universal respect helped Rell make history. In 1975, she became Hawai'i's first female lifeguard, one of the highest ocean accolades Hawai'i has to offer. That wasn't her only contribution to surfing history. She wanted to fulfill a promise she'd made to herself in her younger days when she watched men surf at the Mākaha International Championship: "People from all over the world came out to Mākaha. There were these men, telling these great stories, and I swore then that women could tell these same wonderful stories."

I started [surfing] when I was four, and there were five kids in my family. We competed for one surfboard for about ten years. . . . I'd come down [to Mākaha Beach], and there are like five surrogate fathers on the beach that kind of overlook everyone. They checked us all out and made sure we didn't drown, and we all learned how to surf and we knew we weren't going to drown. It's complete trust in knowing that the other person in your community is caring for you and there for you. That's what Wai'anae is all about. . . . We're here. We're rooted. We're all a part of this land.

My role models were people like Buffalo [Keaulana] and Rabbit Kekai, who really weren't competitors, they just had good fun. You know, lose your board, bodysurf in, and it feels so good, leave your board on the beach and bodysurf a couple more.

—RELL SUNN

The pure pleasure of surfing—it's the one thing that keeps the gleam in your eye and the bounce in your step, and your heart with wings on it.

SURFING MAKES YOU FEEL SPECIAL.

—RELL SUNN

In 1979, Rell was one of the driving forces behind the creation of professional women's surfing. At first, the cash prizes didn't even cover the cost of travel, but as Rell explained, "What surfing enabled me to do is to be a gypsy." By 1982, she was ranked the number-one longboarder in the world. At thirty-two, she was at the peak of her career. Then, while toweling off after a contest, she felt a lump in her breast. The doctors' verdict was breast cancer and one year to live.

What the doctors were unaware of was "Rell time." Her friends knew it all too well. She could be hours or even days late to an appointment. Good waves were usually the reason. She made cancer wait, too. She survived another sixteen years. Surfing was the reason: "You know when life seems to fall apart around you and we are stressed to the max, we take that beach break and surf. . . . 'Yes! We cheated death one more day.' It's what life is all about, when you can just stop everything and say, 'I gotta paddle out and get my head underwater and take that other baptism once again.' . . . You need a beach break. That'll save your life."

Amazingly, she continued to surf professionally for several years. It was in this period that she earned her last nickname—Aunty Rell. In Hawai'i, the younger generation refers to any respected older woman in their community as "aunty." Rell wanted to live up to that ideal—someone who makes the community a better place. Despite chemotherapy and a bone marrow transplant, she worked with the elderly and created a breast cancer awareness program. She brought spare surfboards to the beach, so kids without boards could catch waves, too.

Her most enduring contribution was a surfing event for kids known as the Rell Sunn Menehune Championship. This beloved tradition continues today. Her philosophy was simple: "Nobody loses, everybody wins, everyone gets a prize. It's a great day." In the event's early days, she wanted to give the kids trophies, but had no money to buy them, so she gave the kids the trophies she had won over the course of her career.

RELL AND THE DUKE, THEY HAD SO MUCH IN COMMON.

They were the richest people that we knew. They just never had any money.

—GERRY LOPEZ

Some of the menehune became all-time great surfers, like Carissa Moore, Bethany Hamilton, Sunny Garcia, the Florence brothers, and more. But Rell's true goal was to help people like Duane DeSoto, a Mākaha kid like herself. Mākaha can be a rough neighborhood to grow up in, but a little aloha can make all the difference. "The event holds a special place in my heart," said DeSoto. "[It gave] local youth, like me, a positive outlet and a chance to grow." He went on to become a world longboarding champion, but more importantly, he founded his own organization, Nā Kama Kai, to help children connect with the ocean. Once he had children, he entered them in Rell's contest so they could be menehune, too. Generation after generation. Rooted.

Is it any wonder that when Rell passed away on January 2, 1998, at the age of forty-seven, thousands of people attended her funeral? Her family paddled her ashes out onto the waters of Mākaha, and there they gave "the heart of the sea" back to the sea. In Rell's own words:

"MY PARTING SHOT, ONE LAST THING TO SAY: ONE MORE WAVE, LONG MAY YOU RIDE."

A SURF BUM? I LOVE BEING CALLED THAT. THE MOST STRESSFUL PART OF MY DAY IS [CHOOSING] WHAT BOARD I'M GONNA USE.

—RELL SUNN

Rell Sun Menehune Surf Contest, 2023

RONIN.

ME'E NO HE'E NALU: Surfing Hero

EDDIE AIKAU

(1946–1978)

Eddie Aikau riding Sunset surf break, North Shore, O'ahu

The story of Eddie Aikau has been retold many times in films, TV, theater, books, and at the surfing competition named in his honor, and for good reason. Eddie embodied so much that is admirable about Hawaiian culture and humanity in general.

The Aikau family are descendants of Hewahewa, kahuna nui (main kahuna) to Kamehameha I. At the height of his power, Hewahewa was caretaker of the Waimea Valley of O'ahu. However, after foreigners overthrew the Hawaiian kingdom, the fortunes of Hewahewa and his descendants fell. By the time Edward Ryon Makuahanai Aikau was born in 1946, the Aikaus lived in humble conditions in Maui. Though they lacked money, Eddie and his four siblings had happy childhoods, fishing and playing in the ocean every day.

When Eddie was twelve, the Aikaus moved to Honolulu and found work as caretakers of a Chinese graveyard. City life was a shock to the children, but it offered the ultimate training ground for surfers—Waikīkī. The Aikau kids found discarded plywood and shaped it into paipo boards. Eddie's brother, Clyde, recalled, "If you could stand up on a paipo board, you were king. And Eddie mastered that in six months." When they were ready to graduate to the waves at Queens, they shined shoes until they could afford big-enough boards.

This period coincided with the birth of modern big-wave riding. Californians came to Hawai'i looking for ever-bigger waves, and they brought cameras. It was at an outdoor screening of a Bud Browne surfing movie in Waikīkī that Eddie found his calling—the big waves of Waimea Bay. He was made for it—he had been the family daredevil for as long as anyone could remember.

One of the defining moments in Eddie's life came in 1967. In anticipation of a large swell, big-wave surfers and magazine photographers gathered at Waimea. Eddie showed up as well and, seemingly without fear, launched himself into what onlookers described as the largest waves Waimea had ever seen. In the presence of some of the best surfers in the world, this skinny twenty-one-year-old kid caught the biggest waves of the day, and as the photographers clicked away, he rode them with a smile on his face. The legend of Eddie was born.

Eddie was a stark contrast to that first group of Californian adrenaline jockeys. Greg Noll, one of the first modern big-wave riders, was so thickly built that his nickname was the Bull. Butch Van Artsdalen, the first person to earn the illustrious nickname Mr. Pipeline, was an anarchic six-foot-two former football quarterback. Eddie was smaller, quieter, and reserved, but he came alive in the water. He had an innate intelligence and ability in the ocean. Surfers marveled at how fast he could get through heavy shore breaks. When big swells arrived, he deliberately positioned himself in the most critical part of the largest waves. His calm demeanor in the face of danger was the perfect quality for a lifeguard.

When the state appointed the first lifeguards to the North Shore, they chose Butch and Eddie. Those two men patrolled the famed seven-mile coast by themselves. Nowadays this stretch is watched over by multiple towers and dozens of lifeguards, but on Eddie's watch, not a single person drowned. He made sure of it. When the ocean was so ferocious that their captain, Aloha Kaeo, told them not to go out for a rescue, Eddie went anyway. Exasperated, Kaeo declared that even if he tied a leash to Eddie it wouldn't help because Eddie would still go. This went on to become one of the most iconic sayings in surfing (see The Eddie, page 267).

Eddie was more than a lifeguard. Like his ancestor Hewahewa, he became a caretaker for the growing Waimea community. As the North Shore's reputation spread, it brought in outsiders. The arrival of brash Australian pro surfers created serious tension with the locals. The conflict came to a head when Eddie had to save one of them, Wayne "Rabbit" Bartholomew, from a beating by angry locals. Eddie called for a ho'oponopono—a traditional practice where a mediator brings people together to peacefully resolve a conflict. He commanded so much respect that neither side could say no. Instead of berating the Australians, Eddie explained the Hawaiian perspective—they were the inventors of the sport they all loved but now lived as an oppressed minority in their own land. The Aussies came away understanding their kuleana (see page 140) in the lineup, and peace was restored.

Eddie's growing awareness of his cultural heritage didn't take place in a vacuum. The mid-1970s ushered in the Second Hawaiian Renaissance. The *Hōkūle'a* was its crown jewel (see page 231), and Eddie's dream was to become a crew member. In 1978, he earned a place on the third voyage. He even brought his surfboard so that when they reached Tahiti, he could surf the waves of his ancestors.

The *Hōkūle'a* left Honolulu on March 16. That first night, fifteen miles off Lāna'i, gale-force winds whipped up enormous waves that flipped the canoe. The crew clung to the *Hōkūle'a* all night, but by the morning, many of them were battered, bleeding, and weak from exposure. Eddie was relatively unscathed, so he decided to get help. He hopped on his surfboard, said goodbye to the crew, and began paddling toward land. The last thing the crew saw was Eddie remove his life jacket so he could paddle faster. Several hours later, rescue teams found the *Hōkūle'a* and saved the crew—but Eddie was never seen again.

Nainoa Thompson, the *Hōkūle'a*'s navigator and the last person to say goodbye to Eddie, said, "At a deeper level, Eddie tried to rescue not only the crew of the *Hōkūle'a*, but the dignity and symbolism of the canoe, because he knew it carried the pride of his people. Twenty-five years later, he's still navigating all of us in the voyaging community. He reminds us of what our destination is and why we continue to sail. In the end, Eddie's story is about hope and healing."

But we'll give the last words to Eddie himself. Two weeks before the departure, Eddie told Nainoa: "I need to sail *Hōkūle'a*. I need to go down the road of my ancestors. I need to be in their wake. I need to pull Tahiti out of the sea. Bring back dignity and honor to our kūpuna. And give it to children." And that he did.

Opposite: Eddie was known for looking relaxed on even the fiercest waves. Sunset, O'ahu.

Below: Memorial to Eddie at The Eddie Aikau Big Wave Invitational, 2024

THE EDDIE

When one name is all it takes for people to know who you're talking about, you've reached icon status. Hawai'i has its share of those—Duke and Iz (singer Israel Kamakawiwo'ole). While the Eddie Aikau Big Wave Invitational may be its proper name, the surfing world knows it simply as "The Eddie."

The Eddie is unique for many reasons. It was the first official big-wave surfing contest. After Eddie's death, his brother, Clyde, wanted to create something to honor his memory. In 1984, he collaborated with other big-wave riders to create The Eddie. The first contest took place on Sunset Beach, but then moved to its proper home, Waimea Bay, where the Aikaus have acted as caretakers for generations.

The modern era of big-wave surfing began in Mākaha in the 1950s but grew into maturity on the North Shore. Other surf breaks like Pe'ahi, Mavericks, and Nazaré may get bigger, but when you surf Waimea, you surf history. What Wimbledon is to tennis, Waimea Bay and The Eddie are to big-wave riding—a spiritual home. Part of the contest's mystique comes from the fact that it's so rare. As of 2025, the contest has been running for forty-one years but has taken place only eleven times. This is because The Eddie cannot happen unless the waves are twenty feet or higher, although with Hawai'i's system of wave measurement that means the waves will actually be thirty to forty feet high. This rule acts as a form of quality control. When The Eddie *does* run, the waves won't just be big—they'll be monsters.

The crowd nearly matches the size of the waves. Hawai'i has no shortage of surfing contests, but nothing comes even close for crowd size. In 2023, an estimated fifty thousand people showed up (and sixty-four onlookers had to be rescued because they ignored the lifeguards' warnings).

When the contest window is open—December through February—oceanographers, meteorologists, and surfers monitor the ocean for the right swell. This lends The Eddie an air of providence—the decision over whether the event will run or not belongs to the

I had a conversation with my son about surfing big waves and he goes, "Oh yeah, I wanna surf a big wave so I can get on the front cover of Surfer *magazine." And I kind of scolded him because trying to do it to be famous is going to get you into trouble because when you get into trouble and . . . you're under there twenty, thirty [feet] and there's no way to come up—no way to come up—the only way that you're going to make it through is to dig deep inside where your spirit is and that's what's going to pull you through.*

—CLYDE AIKAU

ocean itself. Out of this came the phrase well-known to the surfing world: "The Bay calls the day."

In 1986, a swell arrived that was so big that it was washing out roads and flooding shoreline homes. The event coordinators debated whether it was too dangerous to hold the contest. When they asked the competitors for their opinion, Mark Foo repeated an in-joke that had circulated the North Shore for years: "Eddie would go." Foo's words inspired the contest to go forward. Not only did "Eddie would go" become the animating philosophy of the contest, it also spawned an industry of bumper stickers, T-shirts, and more bearing that message.

That simple catchphrase speaks to the bravery that's required at every level of surfing. Beginners struggling on one-foot waves will face-plant in the water. Experts get raked over coral on reef breaks. But it requires almost inhuman levels of skill and bravery to slide down waves the size of Waimea's, where you can reach speeds up to forty miles per hour. It's not just the slide, either. If you want to ride those waves, first you have to reach them.

Most big-wave contests around the world use Jet Skis to tow surfers past the break, but The Eddie is "paddle-out only." Getting to the lineup in those conditions is like paddling through a war zone, with waves detonating all around you. It creates a camaraderie that transcends any competition.

Perhaps that is why surfers at The Eddie are chosen by their peers. The Eddie is invitation only—thirty-five men and, starting in 2023, ten women. Unlike pro surf leagues, there are no rules for entry. No points to qualify you, no leaderboard. You simply must be the sort of person that, in the worst conditions possible, other surfers want alongside them. It is this spirit, more than any rules, that makes The Eddie special.

WAIMEA BAY HAS ALWAYS BEEN SACRED. YOU DON'T CONQUER WAIMEA; YOU RESPECT IT.

—CLYDE AIKAU

It's not often that the event director of a contest tells people to ignore the contest. George Downing organized The Eddie for thirty years. In the 1950s and '60s, he was a master big-wave rider and champion surfer, so he knew a little something about being competitive. But when it came to The Eddie, he said, "You have to remind those guys why they're there. We let them know what the importance is . . . remember who [Eddie] was. The man wasn't about surf contests. He was about taking care of one other and the ocean."

It is not just the memory of Eddie that runs through the contest, it is the idea of him. Waimea is a wahi pana, and his life is one of its most beloved stories. His family retells his story each time the contest takes place. It begins before the first surfer even steps foot into the water. Hawaiians are remarkable storytellers, and the Aikau family and The Eddie organizers take great care with the opening ceremonies.

Ritualists invoke akua and thank them. They bless the riders and the boards to protect them. Elders speak to pass down their knowledge and memories to the next generation. Then the storytelling continues out on the ocean in the form of one of The Eddie's most moving rituals—the paddle-out.

Laiana Wong Jr. blessing surfers and boards at
The Eddie opening ceremony

THE LEGEND OF THE EDDIE 'AUMAKUA

There are many moments in the history of The Eddie that have led surfers to feel a greater presence. At Eddie's memorial service, a whale swam through the bay. During the first paddle-out, the bay was calm, but when the surfers formed a circle, a swell passed beneath them, and Clyde caught the wave—a tribute to and from his brother. But it was Clyde's experience during the second contest that made him believe that an 'aumakua watches over The Eddie.

The year before Eddie died, he and Clyde noticed that on big swell days, only one particular turtle would appear in Waimea Bay. They began to joke that it was the spirit of their friend, Jose Angel, a North Shore surfer who died the year before while free-diving. During the second contest, in 1986, Clyde saw two turtles pop up in front of him. "The turtles were saying to me, 'Follow me, follow me.' So I followed these two turtles, and these two turtles took me a hundred feet out past everybody else. When I went out there, the biggest waves of the day came in and I would be right on it, riding it all the way into the shore break." He won.

In 2023, Waimea lifeguard Luke Shepardson was in a similar position in the water:

"I was sitting out the back, and everyone was really pushing themselves deep and I was like, 'I'm not going to mess with that, I don't want to go over the falls.' And I'm sitting there and just right in front of me a giant turtle popped up. A huge one. He popped up and just stared at me and I got the chills. . . . There's a story that Uncle Clyde has told, that . . . he thought it was his brother sending him a message. He went to the area where the turtle was and then he got the winning wave. I was thinking of that when the turtle popped up."

Luke caught the wave of the day and won as well. When Clyde heard Luke's story, he had no doubts. "The turtle was actually showing Luke, 'You're the one, you're the one.'"

The next year, Landon McNamara won and said, "I had a turtle I was following, both heats. To me that was Eddie—and they say Eddie picks the winner."

WE WILL WAIT FOR THAT SPECIAL DAY WHEN THE BAY EXPRESSES ITS BEAUTY—A DAY THAT WOULD STOKE EDDIE.

—EDDIE AIKAU BIG WAVE INVITATIONAL OFFICIAL RULE BOOK

Opposite: Landon McNamara's winning ride, 2025

THE PADDLE-OUT CEREMONY

Some traditions feel like they've always existed. To mourn the passing of a loved one, you gather at the water's edge. You paddle out on surfboards together, form a circle, hold hands, and feel the swell of waves beneath you. You feel the absence of those who can no longer join you. Perhaps a dolphin or turtle passes by, and you feel the presence of something greater. You throw flowers in the middle of the circle, and splash and cheer to reclaim the joy of water that brought you together in the first place. The paddle-out ceremony's simplicity and beauty has made it a deeply moving ritual for surfers or anyone devoted to the ocean.

The paddle-out's origins are relatively modern. Around the turn of the twentieth century, Waikīkī beach boys began paddling out in canoes to mourn the passing of their own. Wally Froiseth, a big-wave surfer and Waikīkī regular, recalled attending a paddle-out ceremony in Waikīkī in the mid-1920s when he was six. He said, "I don't know of any place that did it before Waikīkī."

There are scattered mentions of paddle-outs appearing a little later in California, but like all surfing culture, the practice began to spread in the 1950s and '60s. The boom in surfing's popularity brought greater interest in its traditions, as well as more surfers to mourn. Paddle-outs became a recognized form of commemoration, but they had yet to become well-defined rituals. When Duke Kahanamoku passed away in 1968, thousands lined Waikīkī beach to celebrate his memory, but the paddle-out was mainly canoes; only a handful of people on surfboards ventured out into the water.

At the memorial for Eddie Aikau in 1978, the surfboard paddle-out was much larger. His brother Clyde described that moment: "When we went down to Waimea Bay [after Eddie's death], there were literally five to six thousand people who came down to honor Eddie. The paddle-out is honoring, blessing, paying homage to a person that you dearly respect and love. So that's how we all felt. We *need* to grab

Opposite: Clyde Aikau leading the paddle-out ceremony at The Eddie, 2015

a surfboard, and we need to paddle out to where he rode these tremendous waves." When the Aikau family took out a canoe to place a memorial stone in the bay, over a hundred surfers followed.

The Eddie and its paddle-out became one of the most iconic and visually arresting events in surfing. The idea blossomed and many soon followed. In 2010, people on multiple continents held paddle-outs to honor the passing of Andy Irons, one of the modern era's great surfers. In 2023, three to four thousand people paddled out at Lahaina to commemorate the victims of the town's wildfires. The paddle-out has grown beyond its roots as a mourning ritual. It is now used to organize and protest environmental destruction as well. Surfing can be a solitary pursuit, but the paddle-out reminds us that we are united by our common love for the ocean.

HE LEI POINA ʻOLE KE KEIKI.

A lei never forgotten is the beloved child.

—ʻŌLELO NOʻEAU

When children are small, they wrap their arms around the necks of the loved ones who carry them, so they are often likened to a lei. As children age and become adults, they still remain their parents' and ancestors' beloved lei. This is also why children are also called pua maeʻole, the flower that never wilts.

PRAYER FOR SURF

A POEM BY RYAN OISHI

Lord, by your divine grace, may the surf be epic tomorrow
the way Guy Hagi said on the surf report last night
but not too epic, Lord, head high or smaller please, otherwise I no can handle

Lord, may there be no sharks in the water,
cruising in da surf,
but if get, Lord, please surround me with other surfers
just in case of one shark attack
except of course, Lord, if all da surfers are Hawaiian, or part-Hawaiian, cause a guy
wen tell me that sharks no attack Hawaiians,
(Hawaiians eat fish/ eat Hawaiians/ eat/ fish eat Hawaiians—I heard that
somewhere too, Lord)
but Lord, not too many surfers, please, or else going be like
one H-1 traffic jam, all back up, or more worse,
like Canoes, ho dat place is dangerous,
remember, last summer, Lord, my friend, the skeg wen split his thigh open,
all the way to the bone,
could see the nerves and da fat tissue and everyting spilling out, blood everywhere,
guaranteed had sharks, Lord.
Lord, in that case, maybe couple surfers then,

like da time had da sewage spill after the 40 days of rain and couple
people wen make cause dey wen catch the flesh-eating disease, no not
leprosy, Lord, (blessed be Father Damien)
ho the rain was biblical Lord, you must have been piss off for try and drown us.

Opposite: Daniel Keliihoomalu Kahala Jr. at
Ala Moana Bowls, Waikīkī

Following: Jason Shibata

But remember, Lord, had only me and this other guy,
Lance I tink his name was,
and e-veryting was perfeck,
had choke waves, no more nobody,
just me and Lance
and not too much wind—
ho, Lord, I caught so much waves I could barely lift my arms
afterwards

Lord, may the water not be too cold tomorrow morning
may I wake up early so I can surf dawn patrol
may I not forget the sunblock this time
or da wax
may I not be mistaken for a Japanese tourist.

Lord, tell Fate Yanagi I love her.
May I not be on-call tomorrow at the PK, otherwise I no can go
but hopefully, may I work the day after that so I can pay my car insurance

Lord, May Rasta Jap not be present tomorrow, da guy one asshole,
he take all da waves that fucka, even the shitty ones,
and no share with nobody—
at least he get one shitty car, probably no more car insurance.
Thank you, Lord.
Lord, in your divine wisdom, may they build more luxury condos
along Ala Moana—
no can see da mountains anymore, but da buildings so tall
they block da wind
and da sunsets looks so beautiful in green tinted windows.

KAYAK
KONA
BOYS
love your
mother
797539

ENTERING
TSUNAMI
EVACUATION
AREA

ALOHA STATE
HAWAII
WAIKIKI
ALOHA STATE
HAWAII
HANG LOOSE
ALOHA STATE
HAWAII
HANG LOOSE
ALOHA STATE
HAWAII
SURFER
ALOHA STATE

SLOW DOWN
SURFERS N KEIKI'S
PLAY
808EMPIRE

SHAKA

No matter where you go in the world, if someone is holding a surfboard and getting their picture taken, they will use their free hand to throw a shaka. This simple hand gesture with the thumb and pinkie extended is now universally understood and is as much a part of surf culture as wax and boards. It transcends language and carries as many meanings as the concept of aloha itself: howzit (hello), goodbye, what's up, right on, hang loose, this food is delicious, thanks for letting me merge into traffic, and more.

The geographic origin of the shaka is not in doubt. The Hawai'i state legislature made sure of that in 2024, when it declared the shaka to be the official state hand gesture. Actually, it's the *only* state with an official hand gesture. But how did the shaka originate?

Some people claim it derived from playing marbles as kids, where flicking your thumb is the proper way to shoot. Other stories feature various friends maimed in different ways (shark, dynamite) or someone born with a birth defect where only the thumb and pinkie are present.

The most persuasive origin story comes from Lā'ie, east O'ahu, about a man named Hamana Kalili (1882–1958). Kalili worked at the Kahuku Sugar Mill, feeding sugarcane into a crusher to extract the juice. Sometime around the 1930s, he caught his right hand in the crusher and lost the middle three fingers. After the accident, his employers made him a security guard, stopping kids from joyriding on the sugar train that ran from the factory to Sunset Beach. When he shooed them away, the kids saw his maimed hand and began imitating it to signal when Kalili wasn't around and the coast was clear.

An alternate (and more noble) theory notes that Kalili was a well-respected fisherman and elder in Lā'ie. He led the town's hukilau, where an entire community works together to pull a long, large net to catch fish. In ceremonies to commemorate Hawaiian royalty, Kalili had the honor of playing King Kamehameha I. He also conducted the choir in his local church and raised money for his community. No matter where he went, his right hand was instantly recognizable when he waved. Friends began imitating his wave back to him, and the gesture caught on.

Kalili's descendants actively promote him as the source of the shaka hand gesture, but do not claim the word itself. *Shaka* is not a Hawaiian word because there is no *s* in the Hawaiian alphabet.

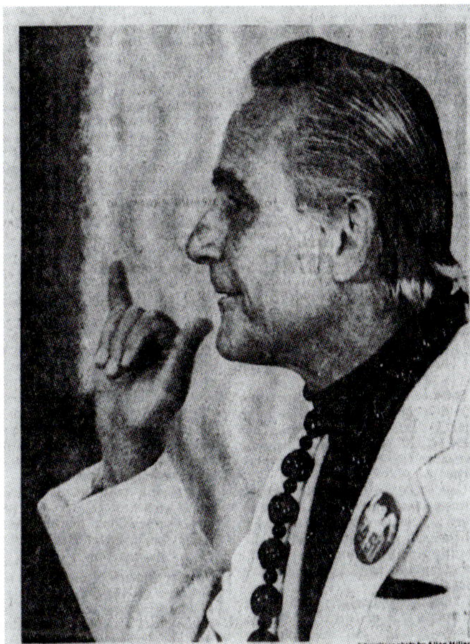

Advertiser photo by Allan Miller

1976: Fasi, openly scornful of Council's Kukui probe, showed up to testify in a kukui nut lei and got sworn in with his "shaka" sign.

So where did *shaka* come from? Some say it has to do with Buddhism, which nineteenth-century Japanese and Chinese immigrants introduced to Hawai'i, and may derive from "Shakyamuni," an honorific for Siddhartha Gautama (aka Buddha). As early as 1877, Hawai'i newspapers shortened this title to "Shaka." Some say (incorrectly) that "Shaka" can be used to bless or express good luck to someone by making the gesture while saying "Shaka."

Here is a more plausible theory. You shake your hand when you do a shaka. *Shaka* is a Hawaiian transliteration of *shake*—like the use of *shaka* in a 1967 ad for Royal Shaka Shaka Pudding, a playful twist on the original name: Shake-A-Pudd'n.

Whatever its origin, by the 1960s, the word and gesture had come together and found modern culture's greatest pre-internet meme creators—late-night commercials. David "Lippy" Espinada was a used car salesman who became a local celebrity due to his fun low-budget commercials, where he spoke pidgin and signed off with his signature hand gesture and "Shaka, brah!" Outside Hawai'i, TV junkies of a certain age might recognize him as the old man who warns the Brady Bunch ("Bad things come to those who touch") that taking a tiki had cursed them. (Greg wipes out in a surf contest! "Honey, do you hurt anywhere?" "Yeah, everywhere!")

Opposite, top: Kalili dressed as Kamehameha I for a pageant

Opposite, bottom: Statue of Kalili in front of the Polynesian Cultural Center in O'ahu

By 1976, the shaka was so famous that Frank Fasi, the longest-serving mayor of Honolulu, made it the symbol of his reelection campaign. Fasi attributed the term *shaka* to a boxing promoter friend, explaining: "I think he meant shake it up, buddy. How's it going? Aloha. Have a good day. All those good meanings. It just meant a world of goodness."

The shaka wasn't so much a surfer thing as it was an ubiquitous part of local Hawaiian culture. But the "hang loose" vibe aligned perfectly with surfing culture. So when Californian and Australian surfers saw Hawaiian surfers flashing shakas to each other on the way in and out of parking lots (and barrels), they took it back home with them, a souvenir from Hawaiian surfing culture. Thus did the Gospel of Shaka spread far and wide.

ALOHA!
E OLA MAU KA PO'E HAWAI'I!
LONG LIVE THE HAWAIIAN PEOPLE!

FILA
FILA
FILA

LU'U I KA 'IKE NALU

DIVE INTO NALU KNOWLEDGE

A LIST OF SUGGESTED READINGS AND NONPROFIT SURFING ORGANIZATIONS WORTHY OF NOTE

AccesSurf Hawai'i. https://www.accessurf.org/.

Ambrose, Greg, compiler. *Stories of Rell Sunn: Queen of Mākaha*. Honolulu: Bess Press, 2010.

Beckwith, Martha Warren. *Hawaiian Mythology*. Honolulu: University of Hawai'i Press, 1976.

Brown, Desoto. *Surfing: Historic Images from Bishop Museum Archives*. Honolulu: Bishop Museum Press, 2006.

Brown, Marie Alohalani. *Facing the Spears of Change: The Life and Legacy of John Papa 'Ī'ī*. Honolulu: University of Hawai'i Press, 2016.

———. *Ka Po'e Mo'o Akua: Hawaiian Reptilian Water Deities*. Honolulu: University of Hawai'i Press, 2020.

Clark, John R. K. *Hawaiian Surfing: Traditions from the Past*. Honolulu: University of Hawai'i Press, 2011.

Coleman, Stuart Holmes. *Eddie Would Go: The Story of Eddie Aikau, Hawaiian Hero and Pioneer of Big Wave Surfing*. New York: St. Martin's Griffin, 2004.

Davis, David. *Waterman: The Life and Times of Duke Kahanamoku*. Lincoln: University of Nebraska Press, 2015.

DeSoto, Duane. *Nā Kama Kai. Keiki Aloha, Kai Aloha*. https://nakamakai.org/.

Finney, Ben, and James D. Houston. *Surfing: A History of the Ancient Hawaiian Sport*. San Francisco: Pomegranate Artbooks, 1966.

HYSDO. Hawai'i Youth Surfing Development Organization. https://hysdo.org/mission/.

Holmes, Tommy. *The Hawaiian Canoe*. Emeryville, CA: Editions Limited, 1993.

Hooulumahiehie. *The Epic Tale of Hi'iakaikapoliopele*. Trans. M. Puakea Nogelmeier. Honolulu: Awaiaulu, 2006.

Low, Sam. *Hawaiki Rising: Hōkūle'a, Nainoa Thompson, and the Hawaiian Renaissance*. Honolulu: University of Hawai'i Press, 2018.

Surf 4 Hugs. http://surf4hugs.com/.

Timmons, Grady. *Waikiki Beachboy*. Madison: University of Wisconsin Press, 1989.

Walker, Isaiah Helekunihi. *Waves of Resistance: Surfing and History in Twentieth-Century Hawai'i*. Honolulu: University of Hawai'i Press, 2011.

MYTHOLOGICAL CHARACTERS

Hawaiian gods are nature deities in that they embody the myriad phenomena—sun, rain, sea, winds, volcano, plants, and animals—that shape and animate the island world of the Hawaiian people. Like nature, they are powerful, unpredictable, and awe-inspiring. Hawaiian mythology has countless stories about gods and heroes. Here are some of them at a glance:

Hainakolo: A heroine known for swimming the entire length of the Hawaiian Island chain with her young son on her back after her husband left her for her sister.

Haumea: An earth goddess whose children embody volcano-related phenomena. Her most famous child is Pele, whose name means *lava*.

Hi'iakaika'alekualono, Hi'iakaika'ale'uweke, and **Hi'iakawāwahilani:** Haumea's daughters who embody gigantic waves.

Hi'iakaikapoliopele: Haumea's youngest daughter and Pele's favorite sister. As a goddess, her function is to revegetate the land after Pele's lava flows, which heals the land. This new vegetation—ferns and 'ōhi'a lehua saplings—emerges from the cracks in the lava.

Hinale: A hīnālea (wrasse) shapeshifter, brother of the mo'o (lizard) goddess Kalamainu'u.

Hinamoa: Kahuna of the surfing heiau Ku'emanu on the shore of Kahalu'u Bay in Kona.

Hina'ōpūhalako'a: Goddess-mother of coral and spiny sea creatures.

Ka'eha: Human brother of the demigod Kaulu.

Kahikilani: Kaua'i ali'i and expert surfer whom a mo'o goddess turned into stone after he betrayed her adopted daughter, Ka'iulani.

Ka'iulani: Adopted daughter of a mo'o goddess (unnamed in the legend).

Kalālākamāhele: A canoe-construction goddess who warned canoe builders which direction a tree would fall so they would not be crushed.

Kalamainu'u: A surfing mo'o whom Kamehameha I worshiped as a goddess of war and politics.

Kamapua'a: A pig-shapeshifter warrior famous for his love-hate relationship with Pele.

Kamohoali'i: Shark son of Haumea who reigns over all other shark gods.

Kanaloa: Supreme ocean god—the master of the ocean, its currents, winds, and all its creatures.

Kāne: In his various forms, he embodies the sun, rain, freshwater, and rainbows (Kāne), lightning (Kāneikauila), thunder (Kānehekili), earthquakes (Kānelūhonua), coral heads (Kānepiliko'a), and more.

Kapō'ulakīna'u: Haumea's daughter who has a wind form, enjoys surfing, and is associated with hula and 'anā'anā, the art of praying people to death.

Kaulu: Son of the forest gods Kūka'ōhi'alaka and Hinaulu'ōhi'a. He rescued his older brother Ka'eha from the spirits who kidnapped him.

Keaukā: Ocean god who embodies an incoming current.

Keaumiki: Ocean god who embodies an outgoing current.

Kihawahine: She was a daughter of the king of Maui, Pi'ilani. Upon her death, she was transfigured into a mo'o and then worshiped as a goddess of war and politics. She was one of Kamehameha I's most important war deities.

Kīlauea: Not to be confused with Kīlauea Crater, Kīlauea is Pele's supernatural hand that remains invisible until called. Pele lent Kīlauea to Hi'iakaikapoliopele when Pele ordered her to retrieve Lohi'au, Pele's human lover, from Kaua'i.

Kū: In his different forms, Kū is associated with fishing (Kū'ula), agriculture (Kūka'ō'ō), war (Kūkā'ilimoku), forests (Kūka'ōhi'alaka), canoe construction (Kūpā'aike'e), and more.

Kūkamaulunuiākea: A gigantic shark of whom Kāne and Kanaloa were very fond. Upon Kūkama's death, they put him in the heavens, where he became a constellation, I'a-lele-i-aka (fish that jumps in the shadow), known elsewhere as the Milky Way.

Lā'ieikawai: A heroine whose husbands betrayed her. She is the granddaughter of the goddess Waka. Upon her death, Lā'ieikawai became a goddess associated with twilight.

Lohi'au: A handsome chief of Kaua'i who was one of Pele's human lovers.

Lono: The god of agriculture associated with noisy winter-related weather phenomena—storm clouds, heavy rain, waterspouts, and rough surf.

Makali'i: A god who embodies the Makali'i star cluster, known elsewhere as the Pleiades.

Māmala: A shark shapeshifter famed for her beauty and surfing skills. Māmala Bay, the old name for Honolulu Harbor, is named for her.

Menehune: Hawai'i's supernatural little people. In one legend, they are the children of Kānelūhonua (god of earthquakes) and Haumea (earth goddess), and thus Pele's siblings.

Nāmakaokaha'i: Pele's older sister who has the power to cause tsunami-like waves. When Pele seduced her husband 'Aukelenuiaīkū, Nāmaka tried to kill Pele. Her tsunami pursued Pele all the way to the Hawaiian Islands, which is how Pele came to live on Hawai'i Island.

'Ouha: A surfing shark shapeshifter who was Māmala's lover until she left him for Kou, a chief.

Pele: A volcano goddess whose most powerful form is lava. Her personality also resembles lava: hot-tempered and relentless when angered.

Pīkoiaka'alalā: A hero famed for his archery skills and whose sisters were rat shapeshifters.

Puna'aikoa'e: He appears in legends as either Pele's husband, a koa'e (tropic bird) shapeshifter who abandons Pele for the mo'o goddess Waka; or a chief whom Kalamainu'u seduced while she was surfing and kept as a prisoner until he escaped.

Punahoa: A beautiful but arrogant surfing chiefess from Hilo. Her favorite surf spot is named after her. Hi'iakaikapoliopele saved Punahoa from a shark while Punahoa was surfing.

Wahine'ōma'o: This chiefess accompanied Hi'iakaikapoliopele's to retrieve Lohi'au.

Waka: A mo'o goddess who appears in several legends. In the story of Lā'ieikawai, Waka is Lā'ieikawai's grandmother who raises her in the hidden forest of 'Ōla'a on Hawai'i Island. In another account, Waka seduced Pele's husband Puna'aikoa'e. This account explains that Ka'ū was once verdant, but when Pele chased Waka and Puna'aikoa'e with her lava flows through that area, it became a vast lava plain.

ACKNOWLEDGMENTS

We acknowledge the importance of Kanaloa—the life-giving ocean that makes surfing possible.

This book is the combined effort of so many people that it is not possible to thank them all individually. But first and foremost, we want to thank the photographers. Surf photographers are some of the greatest visual artists (and athletes) working today, and they have graciously shared with us their images as well as their intimate knowledge of surf breaks. We want to acknowledge the many surfers whose skill and love of the ocean are celebrated in this book. Mahalo.

Special thanks for the work and vision of R. Kikuo Johnson, Tanya McKinnon (agent extraordinaire), Angelin Adams (editor extraordinaire), Mia Johnson (for her phenomenal design), and the rest of the team at Clarkson Potter. We are immensely grateful for the aloha shown to us by Pōhaku and Anne Stone (for sharing their time, home, and tamales), Juice Aguire, Bunky Bakutis, Matthew Patterson, and Jvala and Terry Nolan (our Australian research team). A special mahalo to the incredibly gracious Timothy Tovar DeLaVega and all the other archivists and history buffs who keep cultural knowledge alive—Marilyn Kali at the Outrigger Canoe Club, the staff at the Hawai'i State Archives, Bishop Museum Archives, and Freshwater Surf Life Saving Club.

On a personal note, Ian would like to thank Felipe Dunn (for setting me on the path with my first board), The Ukulele Friends Ohana (for their aloha and 'ike), and Mae Respicio (for her way with words, pro bono). Finally, special thanks to my family for their support, patience with hearing endless surf stories, and for being my ocean companions. Mahalo.

Alohalani would like to recognize the many akua who embody the natural phenomena of the island world and are the foundation of Hawaiian culture and religious traditions, which play an important role in her life.

Nalu authors celebrating the end of writing their book.

While we were working on this book, several beloved members of the Hawai'i surfing community passed away. While it is not possible to acknowledge them all, we wanted to honor at least a few. In the words of Rell Sunn:

"ONE MORE WAVE, LONG MAY YOU RIDE."

Clyde Kalalani Aikau

Lane Davey

Earl "Oa" Kekuanaoa Hind

Fullerton Hopena Kahui Kalanihiapo Pokipala

CREDITS

2–3: courtesy of Hawai'i State Archives
3–4: Turquoise Shadow
6: R. Kikuo Johnson
8–9: mr_tigga
11: James Gay Sawkins
12: Henry C. Bolton, courtesy of Chris Cook
14: Sarah Lee
15: Ha'a Keaulana
16–17: Sean Davey
18–19: Hawai'i State Archives
20–21: Matt Hardy
22–23: Turquoise Shadow
24: Circumnavigation
26: Sean Davey
27: Mike Ito
29 (top left): Sarah Lee
29 (top right): Tomáš Malík
29 (bottom left): Marie Alohalani Brown
29 (bottom right): allou
30–31: Hawai'i State Archives
32: Jackson Kyne Conklin
35: Marie Alohalani Brown
36–37: CJ Kale
37: Mike Ito
38–39: Christa Funk
40: Danny Sepkowski
41: R. Kikuo Johnson
42–43: Sean Davey
44–45 (top): Sean Davey
44–45 (bottom): Mike Ito
47 (top and bottom): Sean Davey
48–49: Sean Davey
51: Erik Aeder
52–53: Neal Miyake
54–55: Sean Davey
56: Wayne Levin
58–59: Turquoise Shadow
60: Christa Funk
61: John Webber, Wellcome Collection
62: Wallis Mackay
63: Brian Bielmann
64: Chronicling America Historic American Newspapers collection
65: Don White
66–67: Erik Aeder
68: Turquoise Shadow
70: Joy Armstrong
71: Brian Bielmann
72: Kalei Nu'uhiwa
73: PB57photos
74–75: Danny Sepkowski
77 (top, bottom left, and bottom right): Kalei Nu'uhiwa
78: R. Kikuo Johnson
79: Sean Davey
80–81: Mike Ito
82: Randy Jay Braun
85: Keoki Saguibo
86–87: Erik Aeder
88–89: Christa Funk
90–91: Erik Aeder
92: Sarah Lee
94: Sarah Lee
95: Anne Stone
96–97: Sarah Lee
98–99: Sarah Lee
100: Mike Ito
101: Hugh Gentry
102: R. Kikuo Johnson
104–5: Mike Ito
106 (top left): Bishop Museum Archives
106 (top right): Christa Funk
106 (bottom left): Theodore Severin, Bishop Museum Archives
106 (bottom right): Anne Stone
107: Erik Aeder
108–9: Bishop Museum Archives
110: Sean Davey
112: Hawai'i State Archives
113: John W. Bookwalter
114–15: Maria Fernanda Bastidas
116: F. Howard
116–17: Hawai'i State Archives
118–19: Christa Funk
120: myshkovsky
120–21: Laurence Hata, Bishop Museum Archives
122–23: Hawai'i State Archives
124–25: Daniel Torobekov
127 (top): Marie Alohalani Brown
127 (bottom): George Burba
128–29: Brian Bielmann
130: John Webber, Wellcome Collection
131: Brian Bielmann
132–33: Tom Blake, Library of Congress
134–35: Daniel Torobekov
136: Maria Fernanda Bastidas
138–39: Turquoise Shadow
140–41: Turquoise Shadow
142–43: Mike Ito
144–45: Keoki Saguibo
146: Keoki Saguibo
148: CJ Kale
149: Don Hurzeler
150–51: Sean Davey
152: Brian Lowry
154–55: Jordan Odom
156: R. Kikuo Johnson
157: Erik Aeder
158: Erik Aeder
160: Daniel Torobekov
162–63: Turquoise Shadow
164: Brian Bielmann
165: Wayne Levin
166: R. Kikuo Johnson
169: Abby Oh
170: DGHayes
171: Louis Choris, Hawai'i State Archives
172: Brian Lowry
175: Joy Armstrong
176: Louis Choris, Hawai'i State Archives
177: R. Kikuo Johnson
178: Don Hurzeler
180–81: Erik Aeder
183: Wayne Levin
184–85: Keoki Saguibo
187: Kal Schultz
188: Greg Vaughn
191: A.R. Gurrey Jr.
192–93: Keoki Saguibo
194: R. Kikuo Johnson
195: CJ Kale

196: courtesy of Timothy Tovar DeLaVega
198 (top): Outrigger Canoe Club
198 (bottom): courtesy of Timothy Tovar DeLaVega
199 (top): Roscoe Perkins, Hawai'i State Archives
199 (bottom): James Jay Williams, courtesy of Timothy Tovar DeLaVega
200: courtesy of Bishop Museum Archives
201: Ray Jerome Baker, courtesy of Timothy Tovar DeLaVega
202 (top left and top right): Outrigger Canoe Club
202 (bottom): Hawai'i State Archives
203 (top, bottom left, and bottom right): Outrigger Canoe Club
205 (top and bottom): courtesy of Timothy Tovar DeLaVega
206–7: Hawai'i State Archives
208: Keoki Saguibo
208–9: Sean Davey
210–11: Warren Roll, courtesy of Jonah Roll
212: Library of Congress
214 (top): *New York Tribune* from the Chronicling America Historic American Newspapers collection
214 (bottom left): National Archives
214 (bottom right): *The Salt Lake Tribune* from the Chronicling America Historic American Newspapers collection
215: courtesy of the State Library of New South Wales, Australia
217 (top left): Library of Congress
217 (top right): courtesy of Bishop Museum Archives
217 (bottom left): Freshwater Surf Life Saving Club, courtesy Timothy Tovar DeLaVega
217 (bottom right): Warren Tong, Bishop Museum Archives
218: courtesy of Spencer Croul, The Croul Family Collection
219: Christian Mueller
220: Christa Funk
221: Ian Lendler
222: Tai Sing Loo, courtesy of Timothy Tovar DeLaVega
223: Outrigger Canoe Club
224: Frank Davey, Bishop Museum Archives
225: Daniel Torobekov
226–27: Jess Loiterton
228: RASimon
230 (left): Kim and Forest Starr
230 (right): Andrew S. Wright, cold-coast.com
231: *Honolulu Advertiser*
232–33: Daniel Torobekov
234–35: Mike Ito
236: Clarence Maki, Surfing Heritage and Culture Center
238: *Honolulu Advertiser*
239 (top): Ian Lendler
239 (second from top): Brian Bielmann
239 (second from bottom): Ian Lendler
239 (bottom): Daniel Torobekov
241 (top): Daniel Torobekov
241 (bottom left): Brian Bielmann
241 (bottom right): Ian Lendler
242–43: Brian Bielmann
243: Brian Bielmann
244–45: Mike Ito
246: Brian Bielmann
249 (top left): courtesy of Timothy Tovar DeLaVega
249 (top right): courtesy of Timothy Tovar DeLaVega
249 (bottom): Outrigger Canoe Club, courtesy of Timothy Tovar DeLaVega
250–51: Matt Cibulka
252–53: Sean Davey
254: Jeff Divine
256–57: Jeff Divine
259: Jeff Divine
260: Mike Ito
261: Mike Ito
262: Jeff Divine
264–65: Jeff Divine
265: Brian Bielmann
266: Kal Schultz
268–69: Kal Schultz
271: Mike Ito
273: Erik Kabik
274: Brian Bielmann
276–77: Mike Ito
278: Daniel Torobekov
280–81: Keoki Saguibo
282 (top and bottom right): Marie Alohalani Brown
282 (bottom left): Theodore Trimmer
283 (top left): Burt Johnson
283 (top right): ArtHouse Studio
283 (bottom): Benjamin DeYoung
284: Guryan
286 (top): courtesy of Brigham Young University–Hawai'i
286 (bottom): Claudine Van Massenhove
287: *Honolulu Advertiser*
288 (top left): Daniel Torobekov
288 (top right and bottom left): Ian Lendler
289 (bottom right): Daniel Torobekov
289 (top left): Daniel Torobekov
289 (top right): ArtHouse Studio
289 (bottom): Sean Davey
290: Daniel Torobekov
294: Ian Lendler
295 (top left): Brian Bielmann
295 (top right): Sean Davey
295 (bottom left): Mike Cerrone
295 (bottom right): Brian Bielmann
296–97: Sean Davey
304: Mitch Meyers

INDEX

Page numbers followed by *fig* indicate photographs and their captions.

I

J

K

CLARKSON POTTER/PUBLISHERS
An imprint of the Crown Publishing Group
A division of Penguin Random House LLC
1745 Broadway
New York, NY 10019
clarksonpotter.com
penguinrandomhouse.com

Verse on pages 35, 76, and 185 translated by Marie Alohalani Brown.

Photo credits are located on page 298

Library of Congress Cataloging-in-Publication Data is on file with the publisher.

ISBN 979-8-217-03460-4
Ebook ISBN 979-8-217-03461-1

Editor: Angelin Adams
Assistant editor: Darian Keels
Art director and designer: Mia Johnson
Production editors: Patricia Shaw and Sohayla Farman
Production: Jessica Heim
Compositors: Merri Ann Morrell and Nick Patton
Copy editor: Nancy Inglis
Proofreaders: Jeff Campbell, Donovan Kūhiō Colleps, Sarah Etinas, and Miriam Taveras
Indexer: Jay Kreider
Publicist: Felix Cruz
Marketer: Emily Hotaling

Manufactured in China

10 9 8 7 6 5 4 3 2 1

First Edition

The authorized representative in the EU for product safety and compliance is Penguin Random House Ireland, Morrison Chambers, 32 Nassau Street, Dublin D02 YH68, Ireland, https://eu-contact.penguin.ie.